25 WALKS

LOCH LOMOND
&
THE TROSSACHS

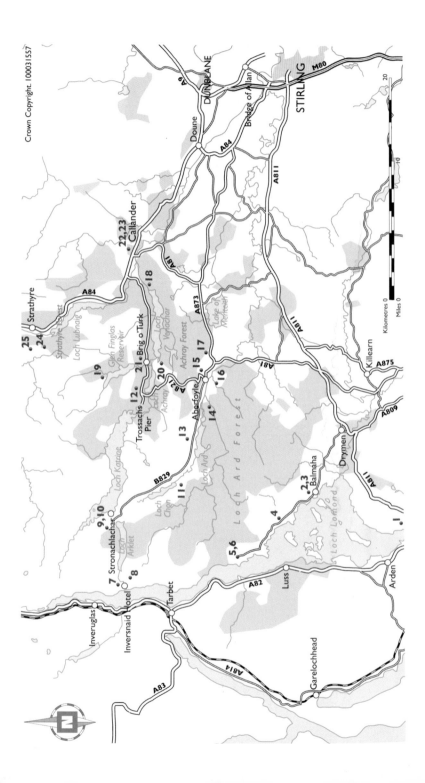

Crown Copyright. 100031557

25 WALKS

LOCH LOMOND & THE TROSSACHS

John Digney & Roger Smith

Series Editor: Roger Smith

mercatpress
www.mercatpress.com

First published 2004 by Mercat Press
10 Coates Crescent, Edinburgh EH3 7AL
© Mercat Press 2004

ISBN: 184183 0526
Printed by Graficas Santamaria, Spain

Acknowledgements

The assistance of staff of the Forestry Commission, Royal Scottish
Forestry Society, National Trust for Scotland and the Woodland
Trust in providing information and advice during the compilation
of this guide is gratefully acknowledged.

The authors would also like to acknowledge the considerable debt
owed to Cameron McNeish, author of the first edition of the guide,
whose splendid work laid the foundation for this revised and
updated version.

Photographs © John Digney & Roger Smith.
'A Misty Morning in Glen Finglas' and 'From Upper Glen Finglas' © Stephen Whitehorn

Cartography by Mapset, Gateshead
Reproduced by permission of Ordnance Survey on behalf of
The Controller of Her Majesty's Stationery Office © Crown Copyright 100031557

All facts have been checked as far as possible but the authors and publisher cannot
be held responsible for any errors, however caused.

CONTENTS

USEFUL INFORMATION

The length of each walk is given in kilometres and miles, but within the text measurements are metric for simplicity. The walks are described in detail and have accompanying maps (study these before you set out) so there should be little chance of getting lost. If you do want a back-up, you will find Ordnance Survey maps on sale locally.

Every care has been taken to make the descriptions and maps as accurate as possible, but the author and publishers can accept no responsibility for errors, however caused. The countryside is always changing and there will inevitably be alterations to some aspects of these walks as time goes by. The publishers and author are happy to receive comments and suggested amendments for future editions.

Visitor Information

Visitor information can be found at the following centres:

Balloch Castle National Park Centre, Balloch Castle Country Park. Tel: 01389 722600 (April-October).

National Park Centre, Balmaha. Tel: 01360 870470 (April-October).

National Park Gateway Centre, Lomond Shores, Balloch G83 8LQ. Tel: 08707 200631, email: info@lochlomond.visitscotland.com (open all year).

Queen Elizabeth Forest Park Visitor Centre, by Aberfoyle (off A821). Tel: 01877 328258 (April-October).

METRIC MEASUREMENTS

At the beginning of each walk, the distance is given in miles and kilometres. Within the text, all measurements are metric for simplicity (OS maps are also now all metric). However, a conversion table might still be useful.

The basic statistic to remember is that one kilometre is five-eighths of a mile. Half a mile is equivalent to 800 metres and a quarter-mile is 400 metres. Below that distance, yards and metres are little different in practical terms.

km	miles
1	0.625
1.6	1
2	1.25
3	1.875
3.2	2
4	2.5
4.8	3
5	3.125
6	3.75
6.4	4
7	4.375
8	5
9	5.625
10	6.25
16	10

Rob Roy and Trossachs Visitor Centre, Ancaster Square, Callander FK17 8ED. Tel: 08707 200628, email info@callander.visitscotland.com (daily March-December, weekends only Jan-Feb).

Trossachs Discovery Centre, Main Street, Aberfoyle. Tel: 08707 200604, email info@aberfoyle.visitscotland.com (daily April-October, weekend only Nov-March).

Trossachs Pier Complex for the SS *Sir Walter Scott* Steamer. Tel: 01877376316.

The Argyll & the Isles, Loch Lomond, Stirling and The Trossachs Tourist Board covers the area of this book, and their website contains a great deal of helpful information. It is at www.visitscottishheartlands.com

The website for the National Park is at: www.lochlomond-trossachs.org, email enquiries to: info@lochlomond-trossachs.org

Further information on forest walks can be obtained from the Forestry Commission, Forest Office, Aberfoyle FK8 3UX, tel: 01877 328383.

Abbreviations

You may find the following abbreviations used in the text.

NTS: The National Trust for Scotland. NTS has in its care over 100 properties of all kinds, ranging from small vernacular cottages and individual landscape features to great houses and large areas of superb mountain country. See also www.nts.org.uk

OS: Ordnance Survey. The OS is our national mapping agency, covering the whole of the UK at various scales. The two scales most frequently used by walkers are 1:25,000 (Explorer maps) and 1:50,000 (Landranger maps). All OS maps are drawn on a grid of kilometre squares. See www.ordsvy.gov.uk

RSPB: Royal Society for the Protection of Birds. The largest conservation body of its kind in the UK. See www.rspb.org.uk

SNH: Scottish Natural Heritage. The government conservation agency in Scotland. Formed in 1992 by a merger of the former Nature Conservancy Council and the Countryside Commission for Scotland, SNH has a remit covering scientific research, habitat conservation, access and recreation. See www.snh.gov.uk

INTRODUCTION

This book replaces an earlier volume which covered just the Trossachs, and the work of its author, Cameron McNeish, in laying a solid groundbase for us to build on is gratefully acknowledged.

In carrying out the revision, the opportunity has been taken to expand the scope of the book to bring in the eastern side of Loch Lomond. This is in line with the dedication of the Loch Lomond and Trossachs area in 2002 as Scotland's first National Park. Not that this book covers the whole of the Park: its boundaries extend northwards to Loch Earn and Crianlarich, and west across Loch Lomond and beyond into Arrochar, Cowal and the Argyll Forest Park.

The 25 walks described here can be said, however, to cover the core of the Park, and certainly if you walk them all you will have enjoyed some of the finest and most historic landscapes not just in the National Park but in the whole of Scotland. This is a much-loved and consequently much visited area. Indeed, tourism in Scotland can be said to have been invented in the Trossachs, and 150 years ago the inhabitants of Callander were complaining at the hordes who thronged their streets in summer. 'Biting the hand that feeds you' comes to mind, and you will find a different attitude today.

Visitors are welcomed, and in terms of recreation are increasingly well catered for. There are hundreds of kilometres of walking and cycling trails, many of them waymarked, and the extensive forests of the area are particularly well equipped in this respect. Full use of these trails has been made in this book, but it does get off the beaten track from time to time. It also includes ascents of the area's most famous mountains, naturally including Ben Lomond.

Several walks encourage use of the public transport links, including the excellent Trossachs Trundler service which is ideal for walkers. The gloriously scenic railway that once ran up through Callander to Strathyre and beyond is gone, but on the positive side, it has been replaced by a walkway and cyclepath which we make good use of.

The area is naturally well served by information centres, and details of these are given in the Useful Information section which precedes this introduction. Let us now try to summarise the area covered by the walks in this book.

Loch Lomond is arguably Scotland's most famous loch, and the Trossachs have been described as 'the Highlands in miniature'. The very name tends to conjure up images of lochs, crag-girt mountains, bluffs and heather hollows, mountain slopes swathed in rich forest and a rich and abundant wildlife—a compressed portrayal of all those qualities which make the Scottish highlands so renowned throughout the world.

But this wasn't always a welcoming land. Before the 19th century, this was a land ruled and dictated to by an ancient Clan system. Travellers were not welcome, and foraging parties of clansmen would regularly raid south into the lowlands on excursions of robbery and mayhem.

And yet, by the time the Jacobite uprisings were over, adventurous travellers were taking advantage of the new-found freedom (and better roads) to penetrate north of the Highland Line without danger. By the time the 19th century came round, the Trossachs were quickly becoming Scotland's first tourist region.

> So wondrous wild, the whole might seem,
> The scenery of a faery dream.

So wrote Sir Walter Scott, one of the first enthusiastic travel writers to visit the area and spread the good news. Others followed, and soon Loch Lomond and the Trossachs were famous at home and abroad. Countless writers, poets, artists and those who just enjoy beautiful places have been drawn to the quiet glens and rugged hills, fascinated by the tales of Rob Roy and the MacGregors.

Today, tourists can enjoy the quiet roads—you can even drive through the solitude of some of the great forests. Many enjoy these forest trails by mountain bike, while others enjoy exploring on foot. And there is plenty to explore. Ancient woodland, modern forests, tranquil lochsides, Victorian industrial architecture and of course the mountain tops, where the eyes can wander over hundreds of miles of gorgeous landscape.

There is history here, and great beauty. We hope you enjoy following these walks as much as we have enjoyed writing them.

John Digney and Roger Smith, 2004

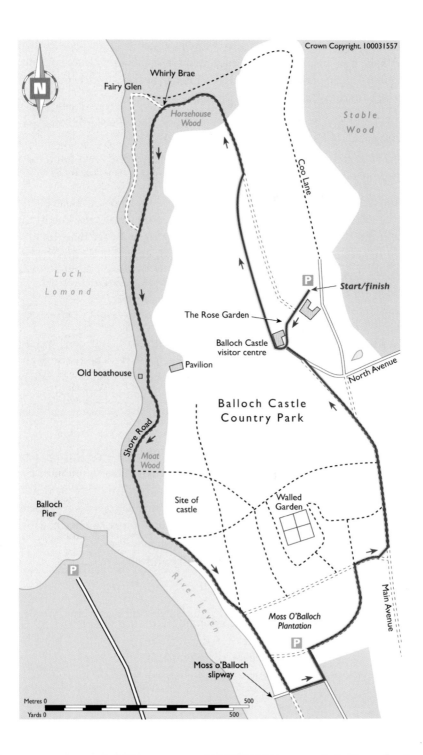

Crown Copyright. 100031557

Whirly Brae

Fairy Glen

Horsehouse Wood

Stable Wood

Coo Lane

Loch Lomond

P   *Start/finish*

The Rose Garden

Balloch Castle visitor centre

Old boathouse

Pavilion

North Avenue

Balloch Castle Country Park

Shore Road

Moat Wood

Balloch Pier

Site of castle

Walled Garden

P

River Leven

Moss O'Balloch Plantation

Main Avenue

P

Moss o'Balloch slipway

Metres 0   500
Yards 0   500

BALLOCH CASTLE COUNTRY PARK

Although this is a short, easy walk, it is an appropriate way to start this book, as it gives you a close look at the southern end of Loch Lomond and also provides the opportunity to visit the National Park Gateway Centre. It is a very popular local walk, and attracts almost as many dogs as people.

From the car park, walk down to Balloch Castle. The Visitor Centre (open Easter to October) has good displays about the loch and the National Park. A map of the Country Park is available, and there are toilets. This is not really a 'castle' but a crenellated house, built in 1808.

Walk round the front of the castle, facing the loch. There is a splendid view across the water, with Cameron House on the far side prominent. Head north on the surfaced path. This is in fact the start of a Tree Trail which includes 23 separate species plus a 'mystery area'! Tree no. 1 is a venerable holm oak outside the building. The name comes from the same root as holly and this is an unusual tree in that it is evergreen.

Opposite a short flight of steps is the second tree, a sweet chestnut. For the full Tree Trail you need to turn right here and explore the garden area, returning to the main path a little further north. The species in the garden include Japanese cedar, yew, weeping holly, and a 'monkey puzzle' or Chilean pine.

Continue north on the main path, passing beech, a pair of sycamores, and a splendid Scots pine. The path bends right and joins another path. The Tree Trail goes back right here, but our walk continues north through the trees of Horsehouse Wood.

INFORMATION

Distance: 3km (2 miles) circular.

Start and finish: Car park at Balloch Castle. Follow the signs to the Country Park from the east end of Balloch and enter the park at the North Lodge.

Terrain: Generally good paths. Boots not essential.

Waymarked: No.

Refreshments: Reasonable choice in Balloch.

Toilets: At the start or in Balloch.

Further Information: Loch Lomond Shores Gateway Centre, tel. 01389 722406, email info@lochlomondshores.com

Note: You can also start the walk from Balloch Station (regular trains from Glasgow). Exit the station, turn right on the main road, cross the river and take the first path on the left to pick up the walk at the slipway.

Balloch Castle and the Holm Oak

The path begins to curve left and descend through dense woodland. In time it levels out and heads south with the loch on the right, still largely hidden by trees. Reach a slipway with a good view of Drumkinnon Tower at the Lomond Shores Centre across the water. Continue beside a fence and walk back into woodland.

The site of the original Balloch Castle is to the left here, but hidden. Virtually nothing remains, though some earthworks can be traced on the ground. The castle was a seat of the Earls of Lennox, the most powerful landowners in the area in the 13th to 15th centuries.

You now have the River Leven on the right. Continue with the main path. Ignore a path to the left and continue close to the river. Reach an open area at the Moss o' Balloch slipway. The river is always busy with boats from the marina, and there is plenty to catch the eye. Ducks paddle hopefully close to the shore, looking for titbits from visitors.

At the slipway, turn left on its access road, and at a junction, turn left to a car parking area. Cross it and at the far right-hand corner take a path which leads back into the woods.

At the next junction, turn right and soon afterwards turn left on the main surfaced path that leads back to the Castle area where you started the walk. The scenery is very pleasant throughout and being slightly elevated, the path gives good views out over the loch.

While in the area, you should visit the National Park Gateway Centre at Lomond Shores. If you have come by car, it is only a short drive and is well signposted. If you came by train, complete the walk back to the station and continue along the main road, following the signs for about 800m to reach the Centre.

There is much to see here and the Centre offers audio-visual displays on Loch Lomond and the National Park. There is an intriguing outdoor sculpture trail, and from the top of the Drumkinnon Tower you get a wonderful view up the loch. You can also take boat trips. The Centre is open all year.

River Leven

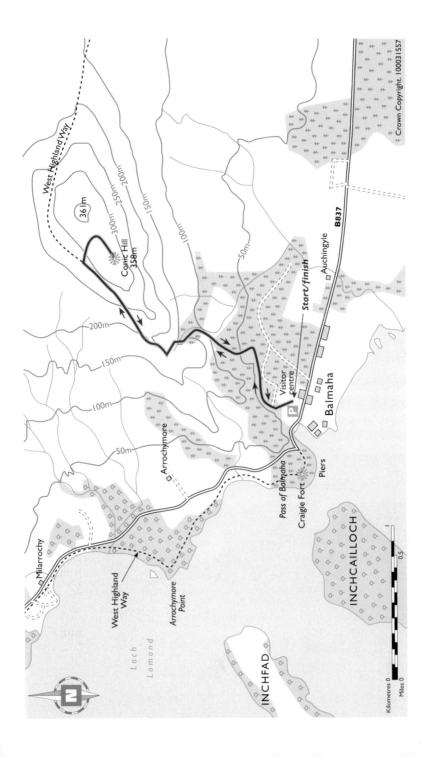

West Highland Way

361m

300m
250m
200m
150m

Conic Hill
358m

200m

150m

100m

50m

Arrochymore

50m

West Highland Way

Milarrochy

Arrochymore Point

Loch Lomond

INCHFAD

INCHCAILLOCH

Pass of Balmaha

Craigie Fort

Piers

Start/finish

Visitor centre

P

Balmaha

Auchingyle

B837

Kilometres 0   0.5
Miles 0

CONIC HILL

This walk takes you to the summit of a prominent little hill which is a notable viewpoint, giving a superb perspective over Loch Lomond, its islands and the surrounding hills. It is a fairly tough and unrelenting ascent for the most part, but the effort is well rewarded.

Leave the car park at Balmaha at its far end and turn right, following West Highland Way signs. The track soon swings left and starts climbing, reasonably gently. At a junction after 300 metres, turn left, still on the West Highland Way (the circular blue trail goes straight on).

The trail is a good surfaced path winding through mixed woodland of birch and conifer. You soon get a glimpse of the hill rearing up ahead, looking almost impossibly steep. Reach the first of a number of flights of steps. The serious climbing starts here.

After more steps, reach a gate marking the transition from forest to open hill. Two long flights of steps and then a stony stretch of path lead to a burn crossing. The path swings over to

INFORMATION

Distance: 5km (3 miles) circular. Ascent 350 metres.

Start and finish: Main car park, Balmaha.

Terrain: Generally good paths. Steep ascent and descent. Boots essential.

Waymarked: Yes (for the West Highland Way).

Refreshments: Reasonable choice in Balmaha.

Toilets: At the start.

Note: You are requested not to take dogs onto Conic Hill.

The West Highland Way on Conic Hill

the north side of the hill here, but a short diversion right leads to a cairn and a fine view of the farmland and woods stretching south to the Campsie Fells.

The path climbs steadily, on a long flagged section. Behind you, the view of the loch and islands is expanding all the time. At the top of this section there is a fine view up the loch, and the summit cone of the hill is clear ahead. The path continues to climb at a steady angle to a point beyond this cone.

The West Highland Way goes straight on. For the summit, take the clear path rising steeply to the right, up to the ridge of Conic Hill. Turn back right for the summit and the full view. It is a wonderful panorama encompassing a wide area, and the islands are especially clear. You are in fact standing on the major fault line which runs north-east across Scotland from Helensburgh across the loch and on to Stonehaven, south of Aberdeen. Conic Hill is actually the edge of the Lowland strata, warped to a steep angle by the fault line. Much of the rock is Old Red Sandstone, as can clearly be seen on the summit ridge.

The name probably does not reflect the shape of the hill, but is more likely derived from the Gaelic *coinneach*, meaning mossy. Sir Walter Scott described the view from here as "one of the most surprising, beautiful and sublime spectacles in nature", and few would disagree. To the south, the Endrick Marshes are clear while to the north Ben Lomond stands proud in front of the crowd of other hills.

Loch Lomond is the largest body of inland water in Britain. It covers over 70 square kilometres and falls to a depth of 190 metres near Inversnaid. The loch is thought to have been formed during the Pleistocene glaciation, and this has led to the loch having two very distinct sections. The southern part, which you overlook from Conic Hill, is wide and relatively shallow, with many islands. Further north, the loch is much narrower, with steeply shelving sides. All this may be of little concern: by common consent, Loch Lomond is one of the most beautiful of all lochs, and its beauty and variety, and the constant appeal it has held over the centuries, is now reflected in its new status as Scotland's first National Park.

The highest point on Conic Hill is actually two humps north (at 361m), but the point where you are standing commands the better view. Because the West Highland Way traverses the hill to its west, you are quite likely to have the summit to yourself as the Way-walkers struggle past with their heavy loads. Further exploration of the hill is possible, but the paths are not waymarked or maintained, and this is therefore left to individual whim.

Return by the same route, back to Balmaha. The settlement, a busy place today with tourists and walkers, is thought to take its name from a fairly obscure early saint called Maha or Mahew, a contemporary of the better-known St Patrick. Not far away there was once a St Maha's Well reputed to have healing powers. Any reviving you may need can be found in the cafés and inn close to the car park.

Loch Lomond Islands
from Conic Hill

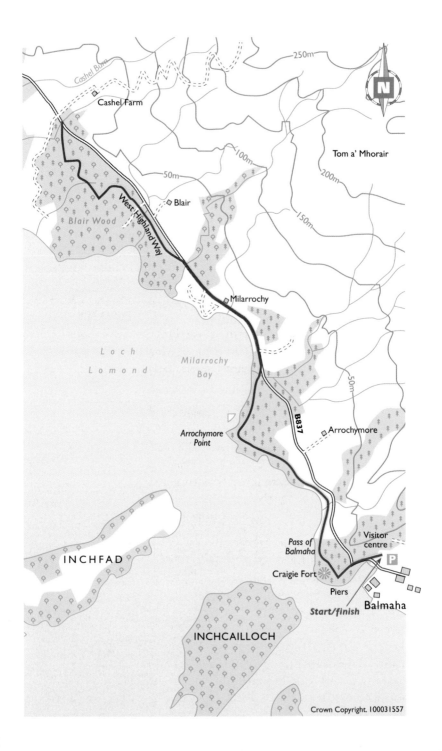

Crown Copyright. 100031557

A LOOK AT THE LOCH

This walk follows the first section of the West Highland Way to run beside Loch Lomond. It is an out-and-back on the same route, but in such lovely scenery that is hardly a drawback.

The walk starts from the main car park at Balmaha, where it is worth visiting the National Park Information Centre before you start. The Centre (open Easter to October) has interesting displays and plenty of information about the area.

To start the walk, go to the end of the car park furthest away from the road and into the woods at the path sign. Turn immediately left on a path contouring round below the hill, noting the Millennium Forest signs. The path passes through mature woodland and then curls down to the road.

Cross with care—this is a busy stretch—and turn right on the boardwalk. There is a viewing platform on the left for the marina, always busy with boats.

Where the road bends sharp right, go straight ahead on the minor road to the old pier. After about 150 metres, turn right up stone steps and climb quite steeply up to the summit of Craigie Fort. There is a superb view of the southern part of the loch and its islands, and northwards to the bulk of Ben Lomond.

Inchcailloch (isle of the old woman) is the nearest. It holds an old church and burial ground and can be visited by boat from Balmaha. St Kentigerna, mother of St Fillan, died here in 743AD. Inchmurrin is the more fertile looking island a little further out in the loch. You are standing on the

Loch and Ben Lomond from Craigie Fort

major fault line that runs right across Scotland and also, of course, passes over Conic Hill (Walk 2, where the geology is explained more fully). There used to be a cairn on Craigie Fort commemorating the official opening of the West Highland Way in October 1980, but it has now been removed.

The southern part of the loch is relatively shallow and has been known to freeze over in severe winters, though not in recent years. At such times the mail to the islands can be taken on foot, provided the ice is thick enough.

From the summit, go left and downhill on more steps and via zigzags, through woodland including some fine oaks, to reach the loch shore. Turn right on the path and follow it round to a small bay popular for bathing in summer. Go through the informal car park and continue, crossing a small burn. In the holiday season there can be an incongruous contrast between the Waywalkers with their boots and big packs and the day visitors, often lightly clad.

Milarrochy Bay

The path winds delightfully along the shore through woods including more old oaks. The loch is surprisingly well hidden in summer. Pass a lovely secluded little beach, go round Arrochymore Point and curve right into Milarrochy Bay. Continue to the car park, information point and toilets. It is

worth noting that you cross the northern edge of
the Boundary Fault here and pass into the Dalriadan
schists and gritstones of the Highlands.

Go through the main car park and down to the
beach. Continue beside the fence and then follow
the path up to the road. Turn left. The road has to
be followed for a short distance as there is no access
through the Camping and Caravanning Club site
on the shore. There is a path beside the road for
part of the way.

Sign at Ben Lomond National
Memorial Park

Turn left into the woods at a sign for the Ben
Lomond National Memorial Park. You are now in
three parks at once! As well as the Memorial Park,
you are of course in the National Park and also in
an outlier of the Queen Elizabeth Forest Park. The
management of the area should be well taken care
of given all these designations.

Follow the path through Blair Wood. Timber from
some of the oaks here was used in 1995 to re-roof
the Great Hall of Stirling Castle, using centuries-
old techniques. Once across the access road for
Critreoch, the path begins a rather tortuous
winding section, passing over a knoll and then
climbing to pass through a double gate in a deer fence.

The ground is more open here and there is a good
view ahead to Ben Lomond and back across the
southern end of the loch. The path switches direction
several times but is always clear. Eventually it passes
through the deer fence again and goes downhill to
cross a burn and reach the road at Cashel. The
Millennium Forest Trust have a base here, and walks
are laid out in the woodland (see Walk 4).

The return is by the same route. You can of course
continue with the West Highland Way as far as you
like, but bear in mind that your route will always
have to be reversed unless you have a willing driver.
There is no public transport along this road. Part
of the return can be short-cut by using the road,
but this is less pleasant than keeping to the path.

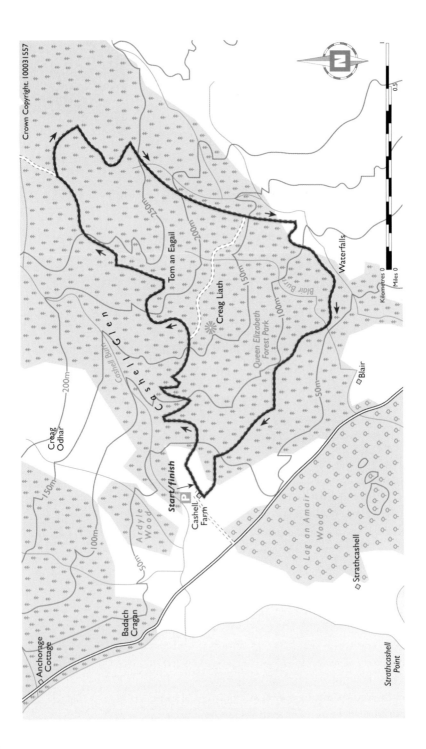

CASHEL MILLENNIUM FOREST

This walk explores the area being developed under the ambitious scheme to create the 'Forest for a Thousand Years' at Cashel. The project aims to "demonstrate the restoration and regeneration of Scotland's native woods through sound forestry practice". It is headed by the Royal Scottish Forestry Society and backed by a large number of other organisations.

The project has received Millennium Lottery Funding, but the Trust running it is encouraging people to contribute by sponsoring trees at £25 each. A dedication can be made with your tree, and by mid-2003 over 3,000 trees had been sponsored in this way. The project website gives further details.

A substantial area of ground has been acquired at Cashel and at the time of writing (summer 2004) there were 27 planting areas to choose from, with a selection of nine species available. As well as Scots pine, these species include rowan, oak and birch. Three waymarked walks are laid out, and the longest of them, which uses green arrows, is described here.

Follow the waymarks through a gateway behind the farm buildings, and walk up the track. You soon see the small numbered arrows denoting planting areas, all of which have attractive names. No. 2 is Red Kite, 3 is Kestrel and so on. Continue with the track as it starts to climb into mixed woodland. A sign to the right points

INFORMATION

Distance: 6.5km (4 miles) circular, with 300 metres ascent.

Start and finish: Cashel Farm, 4km north of Balmaha on the road to Rowardennan.

Terrain: Generally good paths. Boots recommended in wet weather.

Waymarked: Yes.

Refreshments: None on route. Nearest in Balmaha.

Toilets: None on route. Nearest in Balmaha.

Further Information: The Forest for a Thousand Years, RSFS Forest Trust, Balmaha, Drymen G63 0AW, www.cashel.org.uk, tel. 01360 870450.

The 'Robin' planting area

Information board at Cashel Farm

to the 'Donald Dewar Memorial Way', which is part of the short walk loop.

Pass Buzzard and Badger plantings. The views over the loch are now widening. The track climbs in a series of sweeping curves, with each bend opening up new and wider vistas. After a final sharp right-hand bend, the track passes area 9, named for the conservation body, the Friends of Loch Lomond. Appropriately, it commands a lovely view of the loch and islands.

The track settles to a steady gradient and before long the red route leaves to the right. Continue following the green markers on the main track, still climbing. The view is now really broad, so stop as often as you like to enjoy it.

After passing area 12, named Scottish Roots, curve right, continue for a further 200 metres and then leave the track to take the path on the right. Take in the view as this is nearly the highest point of the walk. To the left is the unfrequented Beinn Bhreac (*speckled hill*), which rises to 577m.

Round the next corner, a lovely view southwards opens up. Half right, if you look carefully, the thin pencil of Inverkip Power Station's chimney can be made out with behind it, in clear conditions, the unmistakeable mountain outline of Arran. You can enjoy these views now as the walk is fairly open, but as the trees grow, its character may change.

Soon there is a great view of Conic Hill (Walk 2) dead ahead. The shelf which carries the West Highland Way around the hill is very clear. The path now starts to descend, with new planting to the right and an open aspect left (south). Below to the right you can usually see yachts moored in Milarrochy Bay.

The path curves right, above the Blair Burn, and drops quite steeply before levelling out on a grassier section. There is a fine sweep of heather here, giving a glorious display of colour in late summer and autumn.

Drop down again to reach the junction with the red walk and turn left. Continue downhill with the burn close by for a short time. There are more red than green markers on this section, but you can't go wrong.

Swing away from the burn and level out before dropping again. The view is still good, though it is gradually diminishing. Cross a small burn and continue through young planting. Go through a gap in a stone dyke and climb slightly, beside the dyke, over a low ridge. Leave the dyke and walk down to cross planting areas 20-26.

The blue route now joins in and this section is marked as the Fothergill Way. It leads easily back to the farmhouse and the end of a fine walk. In one of the steading buildings are books containing the dedications for the trees so far donated. Perhaps your name will be there in the future?

View of the Loch over Cashel Farm

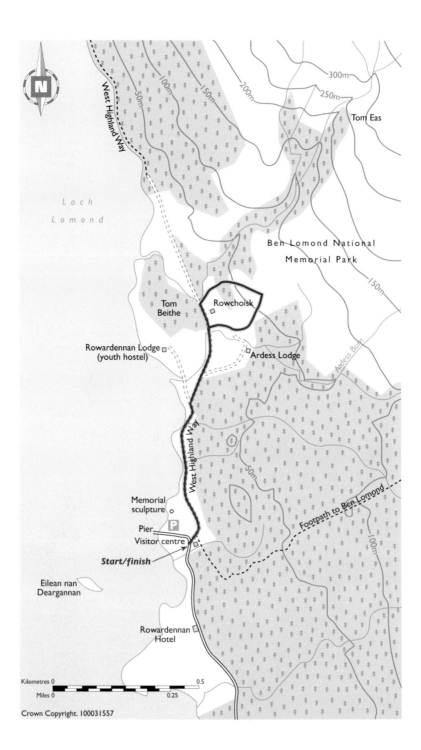

Crown Copyright. 100031557

HIDDEN HISTORY

The central park of this walk is a fascinating little trail developed by the National Trust for Scotland which uncovers some of the archaeology of the woodland around Ardess—the 'Hidden History' of the title. A leaflet on this trail is usually available at Ardess (donation requested). The walk is extended by starting and finishing at Rowardennan.

From the car park, take the lochside path and soon reach the striking memorial commemorating the establishment of the Ben Lomond National Memorial Park in 1996. It commands a beautiful view looking up the loch to the hills on the western side. The Park was set up as "a tribute to those who gave their lives in the service of their country". Great Gable in the Lake District has a similar dedication.

From the memorial, continue with the path round a small bay and up to join the main track (also the West Highland Way). The summit peak of Ptarmigan is straight ahead. Another small bay gives an equally stunning view up the loch.

Pass the entrance to the youth hostel (originally built as a hunting lodge for the Duke of Montrose) and go through a gateway. Continue on the main track to reach the NTS ranger base at Ardess. Turn right to the information board about the trail, and leaflet box.

To start the 'hidden history' trail, go through the gate and walk up the left

INFORMATION

Distance: 4km (2.5 miles) circular.

Start and finish: Car park, Rowardennan.

Terrain: Mostly good paths, some rough ground. Boots or strong shoes recommended.

Waymarked: Yes.

Refreshments: Rowardennan Hotel. Wider choice in Balmaha.

Toilets: At the start.

Note: At the time of writing, there are several high ladder stiles on this walk. It is hoped that by spring 2004 these might be replaced with kissing gates, but while they remain, the walk is perhaps less suitable for small children or dogs.

Memorial commemorating the establishment of Ben Lomond National Memorial Park

side of the house (following white markers). Cross a stile and follow the path to the right. The trail features a series of numbered posts, the first of which is soon reached. It overlooks a stone building below, originally a kennel for hunting dogs used by those staying at the lodge.

Climb to cross a fence by the first ladder stile and then cross a small burn using stepping stones. Point 2, above rushing burns, indicates a former house site, one of a number passed on the walk that show how well populated the area was in former times.

Go left and climb with the path. At the top of the slope go left to another ladder stile and join a rough track, up to a gateway. Cross a burn and continue with the track to point 4. Like point 3, it shows where 'lazy beds' for crops were once worked.

Follow the path (quite rough and wet here) uphill and back to the left. There is a lovely view over the loch as you reach point 5, the remains of turf and stone dykes used for boundaries and to keep livestock out of crop growing areas.

Bridge, Ardess

The path uses stones to cross wet areas and climbs to its highest point, at marker 6. This was an iron smelting site, from the 16th to early 18th centuries. The smelting was done using charcoal from coppiced woodland in the area. Those working here would certainly have enjoyed a fine view of their surroundings.

Soon turn left, downhill, and cross a burn to reach the next ladder stile. Go right to a small plank bridge and follow the trail through the woods to points 7 and 8. The oak woodland here was first planted over 200 years ago by the then landowner, the Duke of Montrose. It is likely that several families were displaced to make room for the trees. The woods were managed by coppicing (regular stem cutting on a 20-year cycle). Point 8 is one of the former house sites.

Waterfall, Ardess

Cross an open, brackeny slope, looking up the loch to Ben Vane, and reach a turf house site (point 9). Cross a ladder stile and re-enter the woods. Cross a larger burn by a footbridge. There are lovely small waterfalls below to the left. Point 10 (a former house appropriately called Tigh an Eas, or *House of the Falls*) is soon followed by 11, also old house sites.

Turn left, cross the final ladder stile, and reach point 12, the remains of a house and steading. It is fascinating to reflect on the way of life of those who lived here and tried to sustain themselves through growing crops and keeping livestock. Despite the beauty of the surroundings, it was far from an easy life.

Reach the path coming down from Ptarmigan, and turn left. Walk down to the burn, with another fine fall to the left, join the main track and stay with it for the walk back to Rowardennan. You can if you wish extend the walk by turning right along the main track to follow the West Highland Way further up the loch. Retrace your steps at any point.

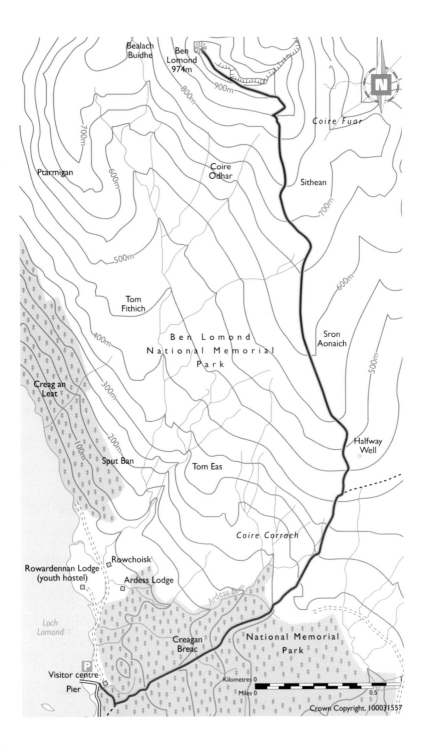

Bealach
Buidhe

Ben
Lomond
974m

Coire Fuar

Ptarmigan

Coire
Odhar

Sithean

Tom
Fithich

Ben Lomond
National Memorial
Park

Sron
Aonaich

Creag an
Leat

Sput Ban

Halfway
Well

Tom Eas

Coire Corrach

Rowchoisk

Rowardennan Lodge
(youth hostel)

Ardess Lodge

Ardess Burn

Loch
Lomond

Creagan
Breac

National Memorial
Park

Visitor centre

Pier

Kilometres 0

Miles 0

0.5

Crown Copyright. 100031557

BEN LOMOND

No book of walks on the Loch Lomond area would be complete without including an ascent of 'the Ben'. It is one of the most popular mountains in Scotland, and is climbed by many people who are not in any sense mountaineers. The path has been much improved, but this is still a genuine hillwalk and you should be equipped accordingly. In winter, of course, it can become a much more serious expedition.

The ascent starts from the car park at Rowardennan, with its striking sculpture marking the Ben Lomond National Memorial Park. This park is a collaborative venture between the National Trust for Scotland and Forest Enterprise, who between them own the Ben and much of the surrounding area. The car park has toilets and an information shelter.

To start the walk, go through the arch of the information centre and follow the well-worn path past the toilets, initially south through the trees, but soon turning left and starting a stiff climb. This section of the path has had a good deal of work carried out on it in recent years but still needs a little care as you negotiate the small rock steps that punctuate it. Take your time—there is no need to hurry.

The slope eases and the path breaks out onto open ground at a gate which also marks the FE/NTS boundary march. The bulk of the hill is now clear ahead. Ben Lomond dominates the eastern shore of the loch, soaring well above any other hill in the area. It is the most southerly Munro (3000ft mountain) in Scotland and is quite frequently saved by those who have the wit and discipline to do so, as the final Munro of the 284—a good place for a party!

The path, which is almost unrecognisable from the morass which existed before NTS

INFORMATION
Distance: 13km (8 miles) circular, with about 900 metres (3000 feet) of ascent.
Start and finish: Rowardennan car park, just past the hotel at the end of the road from Balmaha.
Terrain: Generally good paths. Some sections can be wet, or icy in winter. Boots or strong shoes essential, as are waterproof and windproof clothing, map (OS Landranger sheet 57) and compass, plus food and drink.
Waymarked: No.
Refreshments: Rowardennan Hotel. Wider choice in Balmaha.
Toilets: At the start.

Looking north up Loch Lomond from Rowardennan

began work on the hill nearly 20 years ago, is now carefully aligned and pitched. Please stay on it to avoid eroding the surrounding area. Over £400,000 has been spent on path repair, and the effort continues today. You rise at a steady angle to Sron Aonaich (nose of the ridge) at 577m, and continue climbing almost due north along a broad ridge, the summit now hidden.

As you climb, the view over the loch steadily expands. At about 850m, the path jinks right and then turns sharply left for the final section along a finely narrowing ridge, up to the summit at 974 metres. The view is outstanding. Much of the loch below can be seen, with its pattern of islands punctuating the blue water, while across the far shore the eye is led beyond the scars of the A82 road to rank upon rank of hills.

You may well identify with the feelings of one John Stoddart, who stood here in 1799 and wrote afterwards "it seemed as if I had been transported into a new state of existence, cut off from every meaner association and invisibly united with the surrounding purity and brightness". You might

The view north-west from the summit

even share the unexpected pleasure of the writer of these notes, who after climbing the hill with family and friends on his birthday one dreich November day, was rewarded with a rare Brocken Spectre, in which the watcher's shadow is cast upon the cloud below by the sun breaking through the mist above.

On the northern side of the summit is a steeper face— not quite the "stupendous precipice" that Stoddart described, but a sharp enough slope none the less. There is an alternative route this way, but NTS have asked that it should remain unpublicised.

Return instead by the main path, which is very pleasurable, not least because it is, naturally enough, all downhill. Another early writer, John McCulloch, put our friend Stoddart in his place when in 1811 he said this was "a mere walk of pleasure".

The great thing about the Ben is that it is all these things, and more. It is very much Glasgow's mountain; the whole area has long been, and happily remains, an invaluable 'lung' for the city. Many people from the global Scottish diaspora try to climb Ben Lomond as part of their return to their roots.

Its accessibility and relative ease of ascent also makes the Ben a natural target for organised walks, and each year there is a hillrace, with the winning time only about an hour (yes, up *and* down). NTS and FE try to limit the number of such events, but given the popularity of Ben Lomond, almost every day on the hill is an event of some sort.

Whether you climb Ben Lomond on a summer day when the loch sparkles with sunlight, or in winter when the hill is glazed with snow, the rewards are many. Pick a good day and enjoy it to the full.

The Cobbler and Beinn Narnain

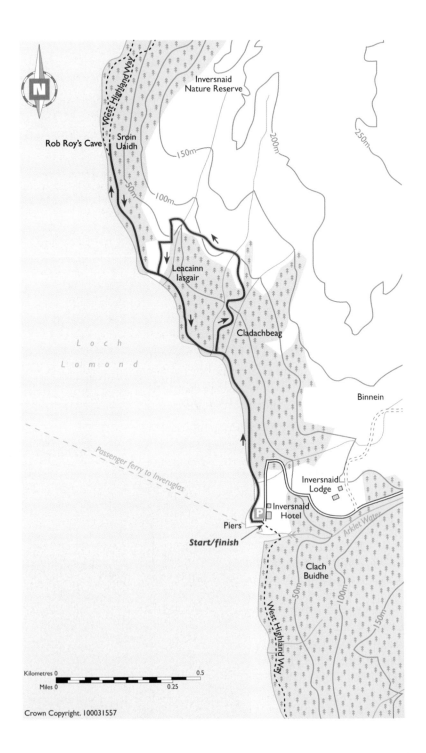

N

Inversnaid
Nature Reserve

West Highland Way

Rob Roy's Cave

Sroin
Uaidh

150m

200m

250m

50m

100m

Leacainn
Iasgair

Cladachbeag

L o c h
L o m o n d

Binnein

Passenger ferry to Inveruglas

Inversnaid
Lodge

Arklet Water

Inversnaid
Hotel

P

Piers

Start/finish

Clach
Buidhe

50m

100m

150m

West Highland Way

Kilometres 0 ———————————— 0.5
Miles 0 ———————————— 0.25

Crown Copyright. 100031557

RSPB NATURE TRAIL & ROB ROY'S CAVE

The road west from Aberfoyle ends at Inversnaid on the shores of Loch Lomond. As you wind down the final steep hill before the hotel, you may well wonder how the present-day Loch Katrine steamer *Sir Walter Scott* made the journey between Inversnaid and Stronachlachar along this road over a century ago.

The steamer was built in 1899 by William Denny at Dumbarton, partly dismantled and transported in pieces by barge up the River Leven and Loch Lomond to Inversnaid. Here the sections were loaded on to horse-drawn carts and taken overland to be re-assembled at Stronachlachar, ready for service in 1900.

There is a large public car park by the Inversnaid Hotel. The building dates from 1820, but it has been greatly extended over the years. In the latter part of the 19th century the hotel became an important point on a popular day-trip by train and steamer. Passengers from Glasgow would go by train to Balloch, then by paddle steamer to Inversnaid and over to Stronachlachar by horse-drawn coach. A sail down Loch Katrine would then be followed by another horse-drawn coach ride over the Duke's Pass to Aberfoyle, and then a train journey back to Glasgow. Even today, some guests arrive by boat as the hotel runs a ferry service across Loch Lomond to Inveruglas.

Leave the public car park to the right, walking north along the shore path through a nature

INFORMATION

Distance: 3.5km (2.2 miles) circular.

Start and finish: Public car park at Inversnaid on east shore of Loch Lomond, reached by taking B829 for 25km from Aberfoyle.

Terrain: Well-made paths. Steep in places, but steps on steepest sections. Rocky near Rob Roy's Cave. Boots recommended.

Waymarked: Yes.

Refreshments: Inversnaid Hotel, Inversnaid Bunkhouse and Coffee Shop.

Toilets: At car park.

The waterfall at Inversnaid

reserve belonging to the Royal Society for the Protection of Birds (RSPB). You are now on the West Highland Way—Scotland's first long distance footpath—opened in 1980 and running 152km from the northern outskirts of Glasgow to Fort William. After 500m you come to a boathouse at a shingle beach. Continue along the path beside the bay, and just before a bridge over a stream the RSPB trail branches off to the right.

Follow this path quite steeply uphill through lovely oakwoods. These woods are home to a colony of feral goats and to a wide variety of birds—no fewer than 115 species have been recorded in the reserve. As the woodland thins out higher up it gives way to open moorland, so there is a range of different habitats to suit different species. The pied flycatcher is one of various species which visit the area in spring and summer, and the RSPB has made efforts to encourage it by placing nestboxes on the trees.

The RSPB acquired the 923 acres that comprised the original reserve in 1986, and the trail was constructed in 1992. More recently the reserve was extended when the Society was able to purchase adjacent land at Garrison Farm.

Inversnaid Hotel and Loch Lomond from the RSPB Trail

The path winds up past the remains of some long-derelict buildings. Well-made steps help on the steepest sections. As you begin to emerge from the trees you come to a small bridge over a tiny stream, and looking back you can see the shapely summit of Ben Lomond. Cross the bridge and after a

short climb you arrive at a grassy platform with a seat, from where you can
enjoy spectacular views over Loch
Lomond and to the group of hills
known as the 'Arrochar Alps'.

Above Rob Roy's Cave

The path winds down back into the
oakwoods to cross another stream at a
footbridge, then passes right through
the moss-covered remains of a ruined
building. Just below here another seat
behind some boulders offers a fine view
across to the hotel in its wooded
setting. The path now descends steeply
to rejoin the West Highland Way. If
you wish to return to the car park from here you
turn left, but Rob Roy's Cave is only 500m to the
right and worth a visit.

Rob Roy MacGregor lived at Inversnaid for many
years, but after he was branded an outlaw he and
his family were evicted from their house, which was
subsequently burnt down. It is said that he used
the cave around this time. As you approach the
site of the cave, the path becomes increasingly rocky
until it threads its way through a jumble of boulders
which fell from the rockface long ago.

You are now right above the cave, but to reach it
you must continue along the path as it descends
steeply towards the shore. Down below, a sign
indicates Rob Roy's Cave to the left along an
obvious path which leads almost to the water's edge.
Here you must scramble over the boulders until you
see above you the word CAVE in white lettering on
a rock. When you reach it you realise that is not a
true cave, but a crevice formed in the boulders—a
good hideout nonetheless.

To return to the car park, follow the West
Highland Way back the way you came, staying
on the path along the loch shore and ignoring
the RSPB trail.

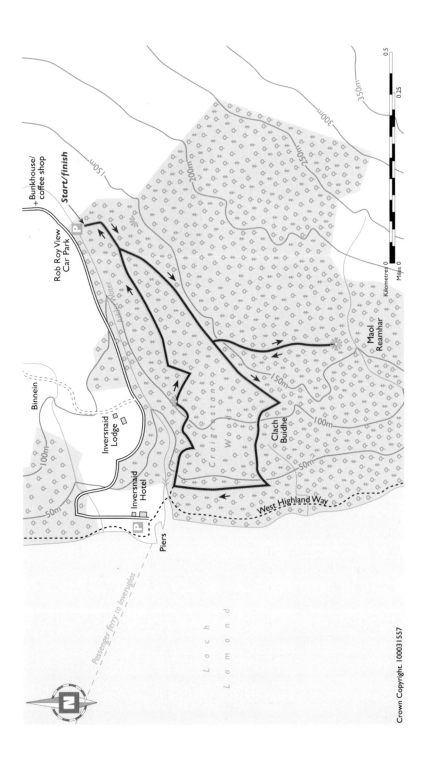

Crown Copyright. 100031557

CRAIGROSTAN WOODS

The banks of Loch Lomond boast some of Scotland's finest remnants of native oak woodland. Although deforestation over the centuries has dramatically reduced the once extensive natural tree cover, and commercial forestry has often choked out surviving remnants, important areas of woodland have remained and are now much cherished for their landscape and amenity value as well as for the wildlife habitat they provide.

The Loch Lomond oakwoods have survived partly because of the steep and rugged nature of the ground, which discouraged felling. However, the economic importance of the woodlands was being exploited by the 17th century when iron smelting began locally. Oak bark was also used in the leather tanning industry, and coppicing, an early form of sustainable woodland management, was adopted here by the mid 18th century. The tree stems were cut and harvested on a rotational basis —new stems would then grow and the cycle would begin again. Coppicing ceased in the early 20th century and the woodlands have been left largely to themselves since then.

As part of the Millennium Forest for Scotland initiative, a regeneration project has been undertaken in the Craigrostan Woods just south of Inversnaid. An area has been enclosed to protect the trees against browsing and grazing, while nearby conifer plantations will not be replaced once harvested.

A short but sometimes steep walk has been

INFORMATION

Distance: 3km
(2 miles) circular.

Start and finish: Rob Roy's View car park, 1.5km west of Loch Arklet dam and 1km east of Inversnaid Hotel.

Terrain: Generally well-made paths, steep in places. Boots preferable.

Waymarked: Yes.

Refreshments: Inversnaid Hotel, Inversnaid Bunkhouse and Coffee Shop.

Toilets: At Inversnaid.

The former Inversnaid Church, now a bunkhouse and coffee shop

A plaque commemorating the Millennium Forest for Scotland Project

waymarked on good paths from the Rob Roy View car park, which is about 1.5km west of the Loch Arklet dam and almost immediately beyond the former Inversnaid Church. The church was converted to an outdoor activities centre in the 1990s by the Boys' Brigade, but has since been sold again and is now run as a bunkhouse and coffee shop.

Leave the car park in a westerly direction on an obvious path across a boardwalk and over a stile in a fence. Just beyond here the path forks and you take the left branch through the conifers. After a few hundred metres the view of Loch Lomond opens out where the path begins to descend, and from this point a detour to a viewpoint leads off to the left and is well worth making, despite the wetter path. The viewpoint is on a knoll offering spectacular views over the loch and to the mountains beyond. The four prominent peaks across the loch are, from left to right, A'Chrois, Beinn Ime, Ben Vane and Ben Vorlich.

On the lower slopes of Ben Vorlich you will see four large pipelines descending to Loch Lomond. These are part of the Loch Sloy hydro-electric scheme, dating from 1950 and by far the most powerful of Scottish Hydro-Electric's such schemes with a generating capacity of 152.5 megawatts. Loch Sloy is situated at 285m between Ben Vane and Ben Vorlich, retained by a dam 56 metres high and 357 metres long.

A system of tunnels and aqueducts diverts water to the loch from far and wide, increasing the natural catchment fivefold. From the loch, the water travels along a 3km tunnel through Ben Vorlich before plummeting down the pipelines to the power station at Inveruglas at a rate of one million gallons per minute. Just to the left of the power station you might be able to pick out

Inveruglas Isle, on which stands the ruins of a castle—a stronghold of the Clan MacFarlane until it was sacked by Oliver Cromwell.

Retrace your steps to the main path and follow it downhill, leaving the conifers behind and entering the protected area of woodland. The path winds quite steeply down, passing the ruined farming community of Clach Buidhe (yellow stones), and descends almost as far as the Inversnaid Hotel on the loch shore.

Just after the hotel comes into view, the path forks and a sign indicates the return route to the Rob Roy View car park, but first it is worth walking down to the two bridges across the Inversnaid Burn to view the falls. Returning to the fork, follow the path uphill. The burn is in a gorge on your left, and further up there are spectacular views of it as the path twists steeply upwards to another fine viewpoint.

Soon after here you re-enter the conifers, but to your left much of the plantation has been selectively felled to open up views of the hills through the remaining birches. Across the valley you can see Garrison Farm, built on the site of the Inversnaid Garrison.

The ruins of Clach Buidhe

The garrison was completed in 1719 as part of an effort to subdue the Highlands following the 1715 Jacobite rebellion. During the second rebellion of 1745 it was partly destroyed by Rob Roy's eldest son, James MacGregor. Plans to rebuild it never materialised and by the end of the century it had fallen into disuse. There is now little to see of the original buildings, which have subsequently been incorporated into the farm steading.

The path now leads easily back to the car park.

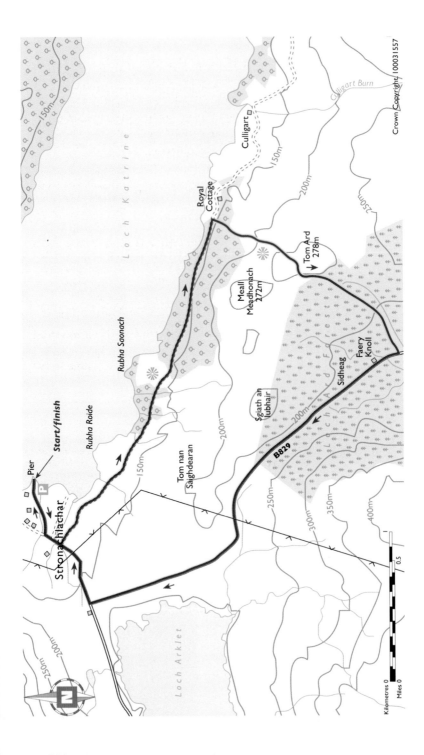

Crown Copyright 100031557

Culligart Burn

Culligart

Royal Cottage

Loch Katrine

Rubha Saonach

Rubha Roide

Pier

Start/finish

Strong hlachar

Tom nan Saighdearan

Meall Meadhonach 272m

Tom Ard 278m

Sgiath an Iubhair

Sidheag

Faery Knoll

Loch Ard Forest

B829

Loch Arklet

150m

200m

250m

150m

200m

250m

300m

350m

400m

200m

250m

150m

Kilometres 0

Miles 0

0.5

1

LOCH KATRINE AQUEDUCT

Although much of this walk is on tarmac, the roads it uses are unlikely to be busy – indeed, one of them is a private road which carries little traffic. The walk takes you through some lovely countryside with spectacular views over Loch Katrine, which provides the water supply for Glasgow. There is the added interest of following the line of the remarkable Victorian aqueduct as it begins its journey to the outskirts of the city, where the water is held in two reservoirs before treatment and distribution.

The tiny island in front of the car park is known as the Factor's Isle, and almost looks man-made as it is enclosed by a wall, but it is natural and was considerably larger before the water level was raised. It is named after the Duke of Montrose's factor, Graham of Killearn, who was held captive here by Rob Roy. The name Stronachlachar means 'stonemason's point'.

Walk back the way you drove in, and about 150m after passing a junction by a bungalow, take the second turning on your left. After 500m you cross the man-made supply channel from Loch Arklet which serves as a feeder to Loch Katrine. The Loch Arklet dam was completed in 1915 and is situated at the west end of the loch, but the supply to Loch Katrine runs from the eastern end through a tunnel to emerge here.

The view now opens out across Loch Katrine, and soon you enter some birchwoods. After the first section of woodland the road

INFORMATION

Distance: 9km
(5.5 miles) circular.

Start and finish:
Stronachlachar Pier,
near west end of Loch
Katrine. Take B829
from Aberfoyle and
after about 18km, go
right at T-junction to
reach the car park at
the pier.

Terrain: Mainly on
tarmac. Middle section
on hill path which may
be boggy in forestry
section, so boots
advisable.

Waymarked: No.

Refreshments: None.

Toilets: At
Stronachlachar Pier.

Water from Loch Arklet
emerges from its tunnel to
tumble into Loch Katrine

climbs a gentle hill. Near the top of this, it is worth walking over to a knoll on your left for the view, above the small headland of Rubha Saonach. From here you can look eastwards down the loch to Ben A'an, with Ben Ledi to its left and Ben Venue peeping over the hillside to the right.

The road re-enters the birchwoods and continues towards Royal Cottage with lovely views down to the water. After about 1km a cattle grid marks the entrance to the grounds of Royal Cottage. Some 30m before this cattle grid, follow a path branching off to the right.

Despite the name, Royal Cottage is a substantial pile, built for the visit of Queen Victoria when she came to declare the Loch Katrine scheme open on 14 October 1859. She sailed here on the steamer *Rob Roy II,* the predecessor to the present vessel *Sir Walter Scott.*

Royal Cottage marks the outflow for Glasgow's water supply. There are two aqueducts, running underground for 18km, the original 1859 one being 42km long with a fall of only 25cm per mile. The second one was added in 1895.

One of the ventilation shafts for the aqueduct

Follow the path uphill with a small stream on your left, which is soon crossed. Immediately after this you ignore a faint path to the left, but keep right up the more obvious stonier path. In a few metres another path goes off to the left, leading to a stone-built tower which is a ventilation shaft for the aqueduct and the first of several such structures you will see on the walk. Ignore this path and continue uphill with the stream on your right. You soon emerge from the woodland through a gap in a fence, and continue uphill across more open ground past the next two ventilation shafts.

The path now winds up to an obelisk with a pointed top. The view from the knoll just above here is superb, with the Arrochar Alps to the west and Ben Lomond further to the left of them. The pointed peak to the left of the north-west tip of Loch Katrine is Ben Lui, one of the highest summits in the National Park at 1130m.

The path now passes the next two shafts, heading for a flat-topped obelisk. These obelisks were markers, built during the construction of the original aqueduct. Beyond it, the path

The view eastwards down Loch Katrine

plunges down a very steep slope, passing through a fence at the bottom and entering a forestry plantation through a broad gap in the trees. At the next ventilation shaft it turns left through a slightly narrower gap. It follows a small stream with a fine view of Ben Lomond ahead, crossing a forestry track and continuing downhill through birchwoods. Eventually it re-enters the conifers for a few metres before joining the B829 where you turn right.

There is little option now but to follow the road back to Stronachlachar. Although you drove along here earlier you will at least have more time to savour the scenery at walking pace, especially the fine view over Loch Arklet to the Arrochar Alps beyond.

Loch Arklet and the peaks of the Arrochar Alps

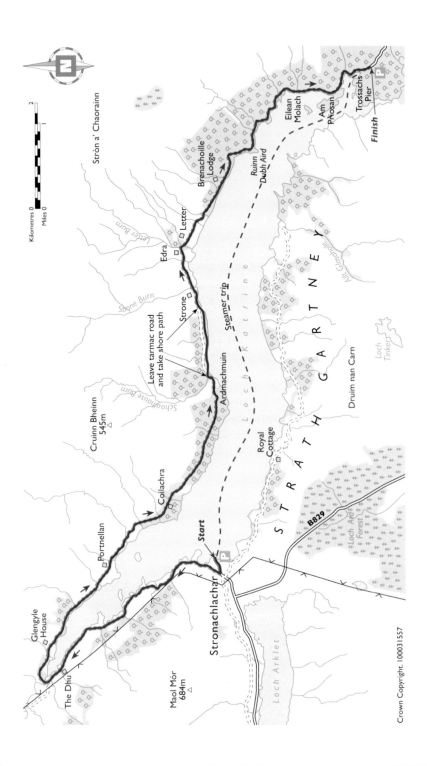

Kilometres 0
Miles 0

Stròn a' Chaorainn

Brenachoille Lodge

Letter

Edra

Stone Burn

Strone

Leave tarmac road and take shore path

Schoolhouse Burn

Ardmachmuin

Cruinn Bheinn 545m

Coilachra

Portnellan

Glengyle House

The Dhu

Maol Mór 684m

Stronachlachar

Start

Loch Katrine

Steamer trip

Ruinn Dubh Aird

Eilean Molach

Am Phrosan

Trossachs Pier

Finish

S T R A T H   G A R T N E Y

Druim nan Carn

Loch Tinker

Allt Gleidsholle

Royal Cottage

B829

Loch Ard Forest

Loch Arklet

Crown Copyright. 100031557

STRONACHLACHAR TO TROSSACHS PIER

This walk has the added attraction of being preceded by a trip down Loch Katrine on the steamer *Sir Walter Scott,* and although the route itself is largely on tarmac, the road it follows is private and carries hardly any traffic. The shores of Loch Katrine are beautifully wooded, and the ever-changing views over its waters to the mountains beyond make this a memorable walk, albeit a fairly long one.

The *Sir Walter Scott* makes three trips per day, but only the morning sailing at 11.00 goes to Stronachlachar. She has been sailing on Loch Katrine for over 100 years, still with her original coal-fired triple-expansion engine, and is the fourth steamer to have served the loch. The first one, the *Gypsy,* was launched in 1843 but was mysteriously scuttled, supposedly by the disgruntled ghillies who had provided the manpower for her predecessor, an eight-oared galley called the *Water Witch.* As Loch Katrine supplies drinking water for Glasgow, scrupulous cleanliness has to be observed in operating the steamer, and conversion to diesel power seems unlikely because of the spillage risk.

INFORMATION

Distance: 18km (11 miles) linear.

Start: Stronachlachar Pier, near west end of Loch Katrine.

Finish: Trossachs Pier (car park).

Terrain: Mainly on tarmac. Boots not essential.

Waymarked: No.

Refreshments: On the boat or at Trossachs Pier.

Toilets: At Stronachlachar Pier and at Trossachs Pier.

Steamer information: 01877 376316

The *Sir Walter Scott* at Trossachs Pier

Disembarking at Stronachlachar, follow the road left past a phone box, and keep left until after some 400 metres you come to a junction by a bungalow. Turn right along the private road. Stronachlachar was once a thriving tourist centre with a hotel, but it is a quiet place now and as you leave it behind you can enjoy the view down the loch to Ben A'an and Ben Venue. The road winds above the shore past lovely bays and islands, with a backdrop of high craggy hills that rise steeply from the opposite shore.

It is about 4km to the north-western tip of the loch, and as you approach it you will see an imposing whitewashed building on the far side. This is Glengyle House, on the site of the birthplace of Rob Roy MacGregor.

Looking east with Ben Venue in the distance

So much has been written about Rob Roy that it is difficult to distinguish between fact and legend, and even his date of birth, commonly given as 1671, is disputed by some authorities. He was a cattle dealer by trade, but was outlawed in dubious circumstances and had a long-running feud with the Duke of Montrose. His defiance of authority and his apparent sympathy for the underprivileged, together with his daring escapades and a capacity for wrong-footing his opponents, have given him a Robin Hood image. He seems to epitomise the independence of the Highlanders before their society and culture was dismantled after the Jacobite rebellions and the battle of Culloden in 1746.

Unless the level of the loch is low, a line of trees standing in the water make an odd sight once you are opposite Glengyle House. They indicate the route of the old road. The water level was raised more than 4 metres in three stages for the public water supply project.

Glen Gyle House—on the site of Rob Roy's birthplace

After you pass Glengyle House, the road climbs well above the shore and gives wonderful views back beyond the head of the loch. Glengyle was until recently one of several sheep-farms operated by the water authority here, but the sheep have been removed following concerns over public health. The intention is to re-stock in smaller numbers once a proposed new water treatment works is built outside Glasgow.

About 2km beyond Glengyle House you pass Portnellan, shortly after which the MacGregors' historic burial ground sits out in the loch at the end of a causeway. Just offshore is Black Isle.

Looking north-west from the MacGregors' burial ground

The MacGregors' burial ground at the end of its causeway

The road descends to cross a stream, after which it climbs steeply for some distance. Ben Lomond comes into view over to your right followed by the Arrochar Alps out to the west above Loch Arklet. You are now opposite Stronachlachar.

A little way on you come to a picnic area at the crest of a hill, with splendid views to the eastern end of the loch. On the opposite shore is Royal Cottage, where the aqueducts begin their 42km journey to the outskirts of Glasgow (Walk 9). Descend a long hill to loch level, and cross a stream known as Schoolhouse Burn. There was indeed a school here when the area held a much greater population.

Only 100 metres further on, you have the option of leaving the tarmac for about 1km and taking a track on the right along the shore. After rejoining the road you pass the three farms at Strone, Edra and Letter, and as you approach Brenachoille Lodge, Ben A'an is dead ahead, looking much more of a peak than it has so far. Ben Venue dominates the view across the loch to the south. About 1km past Brenachoille Lodge, a grassy headland protruding into the loch is a favourite picnic spot, and from here onwards you are likely to see more people on the road, as many walkers and cyclists from Trossachs Pier come this far before turning back.

In a further 1 km you pass the Silver Strand, once a white pebbly beach but now submerged, although still marked on some maps. Opposite is Eilean Molach, the largest of three wooded islands. Here the doughty Helen Stewart, hiding with other women and their children, decapitated one of Cromwell's soldiers who had had the audacity to swim across to them. In Sir Walter Scott's *Lady of the Lake*, the island was the refuge of the heroine, Ellen Douglas, and is now known as Ellen's Isle.

The road now follows a ledge hewn out of the steep crags that hem in this eastern end of the loch, following every twist of the shoreline except where it crosses the neck of the peninsula Am Priosan—the Prison. It is now only a short distance to Trossachs Pier and its facilities.

The view across the loch, near to Trossachs Pier

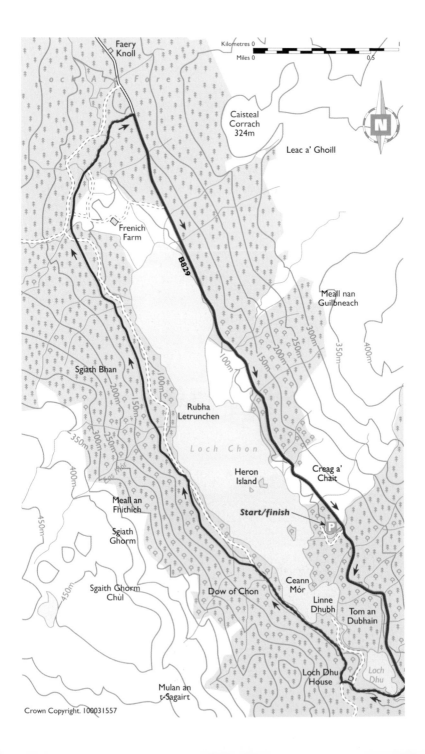

Faery
Knoll

Caisteal
Corrach
324m

Leac a' Ghoill

Frenich
Farm

B829

Meall nan
Guilbneach

300m

250m

200m

350m

400m

Sgiath Bhan

150m

100m

200m

150m

100m

Rubha
Letrunchen

350m

300m

250m

400m

Loch Chon

Heron
Island

Creag a'
Chait

Meall an
Fhithich

Start/finish

P

Sgiath
Ghorm

450m

Sgaith Ghorm
Chùl

Dow of Chon

Ceann
Mór

Linne
Dhubh

Tom an
Dubhain

450m

Mulan an
t-Sagairt

Loch Dhu
House

Loch
Dhu

Kilometres 0
Miles 0   0.5

N

Crown Copyright. 100031557

LOCHS DHU & CHON

This walk includes about 4km along the B829, but by parking at the Forestry Commission's Loch Chon car park you can cover some of this distance at the start and so reduce the amount of road walking at the end. In any case, the road is fairly quiet and the views from it across the loch are very fine.

The middle section of the walk follows an old path along the line of the Loch Katrine aqueduct, which is hidden below you in its tunnel for much of the time, but occasionally surfacing where it has to span the gullies of the larger streams feeding Loch Chon. The name means *loch of the dog*, after a legendary dog-like water-monster that is reputed to inhabit its dark waters. Even if the monster decides to show itself you may well miss it, as the views from this path are much restricted by the forestry through which it threads. However, the path itself is for the most part firm and dry and well worth walking for its own sake.

From the car park, walk back along the road about 1km to Loch Dhu—the Black Loch. At its far end, take a track on the right leading to the buildings of

INFORMATION

Distance: 10km (6 miles) circular.

Start and finish: Forestry Commission car park on B829, near southern end of Loch Chon.

Terrain: Good paths, forestry tracks and a section on the B829 road. Boots needed in wet conditions.

Waymarked: No.

Refreshments: None.

Toilets: None on route.

Loch Chon from the car park

Loch Dhu

Loch Dhu House, just beyond which you turn sharp right on to a wide forestry track. This leads to the southern tip of Loch Chon, and follows its shore for a few hundred metres before swinging away from the loch up a gentle rise.

At the very top of this rise, a small cairn on the left marks the point where the footpath branches off. Even if you don't spot the cairn you should be able to see the path ahead, and for much of the length of the loch it runs parallel with the forestry track and only a short distance above it. The path initially crosses an area where the forestry has been felled, and partway across here you can see the aqueduct where it emerges between two sections of tunnel to bridge a gully by means of a metal conduit.

The path now plunges into the forestry – further felling is due to take place on this hillside but path diversions will normally be indicated. In a few hundred metres you pass a lattice-domed ventilation shaft, the first of several. The path continues through the trees with glimpses of the loch. A little further on, just by a short stone post, it slants down to merge with the forestry track which you must now join for about 100 metres.

One of the lattice-domed ventilation shafts

The best place to regain the path is just past some gabions (wire baskets filled with stones) forming the embankment. At the end of these, a small stream runs down a man-made channel. Cross it and follow its bank uphill for a few paces, and immediately on re-entering the trees you can discern the path leading away to the right. It is rather faint to begin with, but soon re-asserts itself after crossing another small stream.

The path undulates and soon passes another lattice-domed shaft. Further on, two grids at ground level serve as reminders that you are right over the original aqueduct, and you can peer down and see the water flowing silently below. The echo is good too! You then pass a blocked-up tunnel in the rocks and two more sections of conduit. Beside the second one, a metal bridge leads you out of the forestry and to open ground more or less level with the end of the loch.

In a few hundred metres, the path crosses the forestry track just by another lattice-domed shaft, then continues over a bridge across a cascading stream and up through a small gate, with Frenich Farm over to your right. After crossing a larger man-made channel it enters the forest through a broad ride which soon leads to a fenced area with yet another lattice-domed shaft. Here the path joins a vehicle track which winds up the hillside below yet another shaft, this time without a dome, to join the B829 road where you go right.

Once you reach Loch Chon again, it might seem tempting to follow its shore in order to avoid the road walking, but this is barely worthwhile as the going is rough and wet in places. You may as well stay on the road and enjoy the views down to the loch.

The northern end of Loch Chon

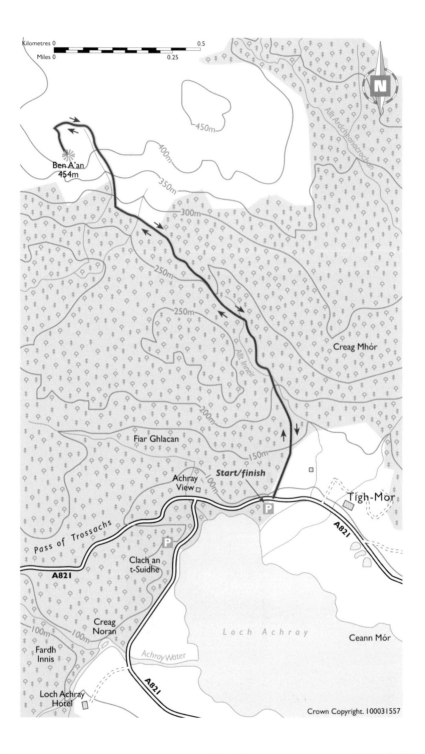

Kilometres 0   0.5
Miles 0   0.25

N

450m
400m
350m
300m
250m
250m
200m
150m
100m
100m
100m

Ben A'an
454m

Allt Ard-choineachain

Creag Mhór

Allt Inneir

Fiar Ghlacan

Achray
View

Start/finish

Tìgh-Mór

A821

Pass of Trossachs

A821

Clach an
t-Suidhe

Creag
Noran

Loch Achray

Ceann Mór

Fardh
Innis

Achray Water

A821

Loch Achray
Hotel

Crown Copyright. 100031557

BEN A'AN

Although only 454m in height, the rocky cone of Ben A'an dominates the view from the southern shores of Loch Achray, and its ascent is probably the most popular hill-walk in the Trossachs. From some other angles it can be seen that the summit is only a spur of the high moorland area culminating in Meall Gainmheich to the north, but the intervening ground dips just sufficiently for Ben A'an to feel like a separate hill, and its rocky southern slopes certainly give it the feel of a miniature mountain.

In fact, there is enough exposed rock for Ben A'an to have attracted climbers and a variety of short routes have been established over the years. But the route to the summit described here, although steep and rocky in places, is straightforward enough in fine weather and is an excellent introduction to hillwalking for children.

This is the true heart of the Trossachs. The name is generally supposed to mean "bristly country" and refers to the tangle of small wooded hills in the pass between Loch Achray and Loch Katrine, but it is now loosely applied to the whole surrounding area. Even the name Ben A'an is spurious—it was contrived by Sir Walter Scott in his poem *The Lady of the Lake* and has stuck. The true name is Binnein.

Ben A'an has its own car park, situated near the north-west tip of Loch Achray only a few hundred metres east of the road junction for Trossachs Pier. To begin the walk, cross

INFORMATION

Distance: 6km (4 miles) circular, with 350m ascent.

Start and finish: Ben A'an car park near north west tip of Loch Achray, just east of A821 junction to Trossachs Pier.

Terrain: Generally well-maintained path, but steep for much of the way and rocky towards the top. Boots essential.

Waymarked: At start.

Refreshments: At Trossachs Pier and Loch Achray Hotel.

Toilets: At Trossachs Pier.

Ben A'an from Loch Achray

The summit from the half-way point

the road and follow the well-marked path uphill alongside the forest edge.

The grandiose building over to your right is the former Trossachs Hotel, sadly run-down for some years but now renovated and extended, and enjoying a new lease of life as a Holiday Property Bond establishment under the name of Tigh Mor (*big house*). Its splendid 'candlesnuffer' turrets are imitated on the modern house further up the hillside.

The path climbs steeply through the larches, but levels out briefly where it runs above a stream before steepening again to cross the stream by a bridge. A further steep section follows before the path levels off completely. Here you can walk out to a viewpoint on the left, where a rocky outcrop offers glimpses of the summit of Ben A'an, and in the other direction a view down to Loch Achray.

The path now runs level for a short distance, re-crosses the stream and undulates, eventually rising gently to emerge from the larches, where you are rewarded with a superb view of the peak directly ahead.

The ground becomes much more open here, and although the main path goes straight ahead, it is worth wandering over to the left on another path immediately as you come out of the larches. This leads to a grassy area from where there are wonderful views of Ben Venue and glimpses of Loch Katrine through the scattered birchwoods.

You return to the main path, which leads through birches up to another grassy area directly below the summit cone, where some boulders provide a good resting-place before tackling the ascent. The path now heads straight up, becoming much steeper and rockier. Excellent restoration work means that it should present no problem unless under snow or ice, although after crossing a stream it becomes rather looser and more eroded.

Some distance further up, two paths branch off steeply to the left and converge beneath the summit crags to form an alternative route to the top, but it is probably best to ignore them and continue straight ahead. Eventually, the path levels off and sweeps round to the left to make the final short climb to the rocky summit.

Not surprisingly, the view from the top is magnificent. Ben Venue dominates to the south-west across the eastern end of Loch Katrine. Loch Achray and Loch Venachar lie to its left, and further round to the east is the bulk of Ben Ledi. However, it is the view west down the length of Loch Katrine that will really catch the eye. The very end of the loch is hidden as it snakes to the right, but the buildings of Stronachlachar are easily visible in clear weather.

To the left of here the Arrochar Alps line up on the horizon, while to the right the Crianlarich hills culminate in the twin peaks of Ben More and Stobinian, the highest summits in Loch Lomond and the Trossachs National Park. Indeed, at 1174m, Ben More is the 15th highest mountain in Scotland.

Return by the same route, taking care as you descend the steep ground.

The view down
Loch Katrine
from the summit

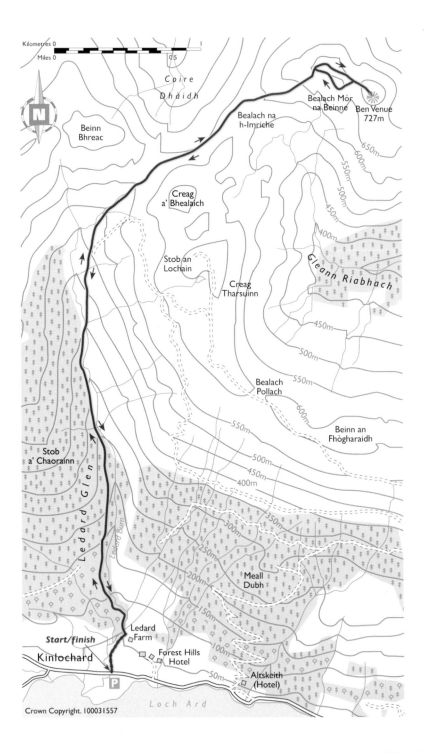

BEN VENUE

Ben Venue can be climbed from Loch Achray, but the alternatives from that side involve either a long approach through forestry or relying on indistinct paths over rough ground. The preferable approach described here is from Loch Ard to the south, even though the going can in places be quite wet.

Park in the lay-by opposite Ledard Farm, just west of Forest Hills Hotel. Cross the road and walk up the farm track beside the stream. Just before reaching the farm buildings, leave the track to go over a stile and then cross the burn by a footbridge. The path climbs through oakwoods, soon passing a lovely waterfall which so impressed Sir Walter Scott that he wrote of it "I never saw anything which I admired so much: the height is not remarkable, but the accompaniments are exquisitely beautiful".

The oakwoods give way to birch a little higher up, with a forestry plantation on the left. A short boggy section of some 80 metres is avoided by crossing briefly in and out of the plantation by means of two stiles that have been provided for the purpose. The path now continues up to enter the birches, narrowing as it clings to the hillside with the Ledard Burn rushing through its ravine well below you.

Some way on, at a fork in the path, a sign requests that you take the left branch. Above here there are a few boggy sections as the path threads its way through the trees, eventually emerging from them to join a wider track which leads up to a point where you cross the burn. This is a good spot to sit and enjoy the view. The

INFORMATION

Distance: 11km (7 miles) circular, with 700m ascent.

Start and finish: Lay-by opposite Ledard Farm, 500 metres east of Kinlochard.

Terrain: Clear path most of the way, but a number of boggy sections. The walk should only be undertaken in good conditions unless you are an experienced hillwalker. Boots essential, and adequate spare clothing, food and drink, map (OS Landranger sheet 57) and compass should be carried.

Waymarked: In places.

Refreshments: Forest Hills Hotel and Altskeith Hotel, both just east of starting point.

Toilets: None in area.

Ben Venue from Loch Achray

rocky hill ahead is Beinn Bhreac (*speckled peak*) – Ben Venue is still hidden over to its right.

After crossing the burn you climb a ladder stile over a deer fence and about 150 metres further on, look out for a junction of paths where you go right. It is easy to miss this, as the more likely looking path is the one leading straight ahead, but the higher one to the right is drier. The lower one crosses and re-crosses the fence, but if you find yourself on it don't worry, as the two paths join further up.

Ledard Farm at the start of the walk

Another boggy section is negotiated before the path follows one of the tributaries of the Ledard Burn and levels out at the saddle below Beinn Bhreac, where you cross the fence by a stile. Here you get your first sight of Ben Venue. There are two summits, the left-hand one being slightly higher, although the right-hand one has the triangulation pillar. The path now runs level, even descending slightly, with wonderful views opening out down to Loch Katrine and the impressive peak of Stobinian dominating beyond.

After rounding one or two rocky outcrops, the path begins to rise again. A brief descent leads to a cairn where the path from Loch Achray joins in from the right, and from here a steep, loose section of path leads to a line of old fence posts. There are now fine views behind to Ben Lomond and the Arrochar Alps. A short boggy section is followed by another steep climb, beyond which there is a sharp dip. Here the path forks—the right branch leads to the right-hand summit and you can return by this path if you choose to visit both tops. But for now, stay to the left and follow the path as it leads round the dip and up the final rocky slopes to the first summit.

This is a wonderful vantage point by any standards. If the weather is fine, you will want to spend some time here to enjoy the panorama, and it is worth wandering a short distance from the cairn for the full-length view of Loch Katrine. At its wooded eastern end, the largest island is Ellen's Isle, so named by Sir Walter Scott in *The Lady of the Lake.* Opposite this on the near shore is Coire na Uruisgean, or corrie of the goblins – reputed to be their favoured meeting place. To the south the Isle of Arran is visible on a clear day, and through the gap to the right of the Campsie Fells you can see well into the Southern Uplands.

You can now return the way you came, or if you are a purist and wish to visit the second top it will only add a few minutes to the walk. The path across to it more or less follows the old fence posts, and drops to a gap beyond which it climbs below a prominent buttress towards the top. Just before descending to this gap, you will notice a path coming in from the right. You can use this path on your return to avoid having to re-ascend the first top, but for now you continue below the buttress up to the trig point. The view is slightly less good than from the first top, which from here blocks much of the view along Loch Katrine.

Beside the Ledard Burn

Looking north-west along the length of Loch Katrine from near the summit

To return, descend to the gap and climb up a short way to locate the fork in the path where you go left to contour round the first top. Descend a rather wet grassy slope, beyond which the path swings right to rejoin the main route. This is followed all the way back to the start of the walk.

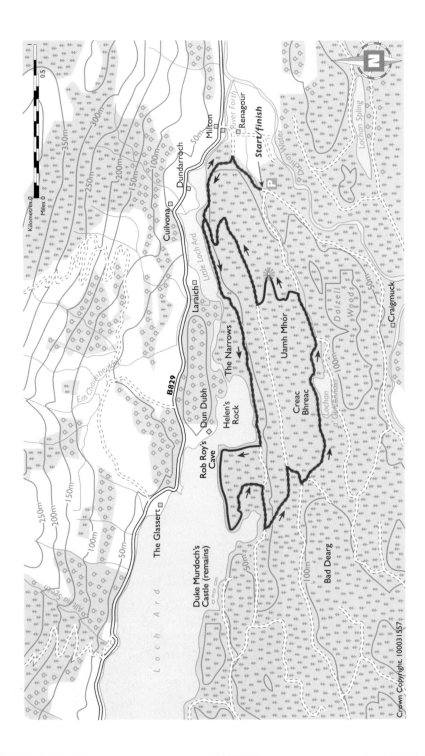

Kilometres 0
Miles 0
0.5

N

300m
350m
250m
200m
150m
100m
50m

Milton
River Forth
Renagour
Start/finish
P
Dundarroch
Cuilvona
Daichlay Water
Little Loch Ard
Lochan Spling
Laraich
The Narrows
Uamh Mhòr
Dalzell Wood
Craigmuck
B829
Dun Dubh
Helen's Rock
Creac Bhreac
100m
Lochan Gleann mor
Rob Roy's Cave
50m
Bad Dearg
100m
The Glassert
Duke Murdoch's Castle (remains)
50m
Eas Chrainbheinn
Allt na Sessia
150m
200m
250m
L o c h   A r d

Crown Copyright. 100031557

LOCH ARD

The conservation area of Milton lies about 2 km west of Aberfoyle, and has several beautifully restored cottages. As you approach travelling west along the B829, the first cottage on the left has a post-box set into its wall. Turn left down a lane immediately before this cottage, cross a bridge, fork right, then left following signs to a Forestry Commission car park.

Walk back to the fork where you turned left, then go left again to follow the track to Little Loch Ard (or Lower Loch Ard) which is really two lochans joined by a channel through the reeds, and linked to Loch Ard itself by a short section of slow-flowing river. At the end of the first lochan a track branches uphill to the left—this is your return route—but for now you continue beside the shore.

Loch Ard can claim to be the most attractive and fascinating of the Trossachs lochs, with its quiet bays, backwaters and islands. The view westwards down its length is dominated by Ben Lomond and is a favourite for many photographers and artists.

The semi-natural oakwoods on the opposite shore are protected as a Site of Special Scientific Interest, and often form lovely reflections in the sheltered water. At the end of the second locha, the track swings uphill with glimpses of Ben Lomond beyond the meandering stream. This section is hidden from the B829,

INFORMATION

Distance: 9km (5.5 miles) circular.

Start and finish: Forestry Commission car park at Milton. About 2km west of Aberfoyle on B829, turn left down a lane immediately before the first cottage on the left. Follow signs to car park.

Terrain: Forestry tracks and purpose-built paths. Boots not essential.

Waymarked: In places.

Refreshments: Good choice in Aberfoyle.

Toilets: In Aberfoyle.

Loch Ard and the tiny islet of Dundochil

and you may see heron and a variety of ducks such as goosander, pochard, tufted duck and mallard.

After 500m the track descends to the water's edge at the eastern end of Loch Ard itself. On the opposite shore a conspicuous outcrop is known as Helen's Rock—named after Rob Roy's wife who was called Helen by Sir Walter Scott in his novel, *Rob Roy*. She allegedly threw an exciseman into the water from here, having first tied him up and weighed him down with a heavy stone.

After a few hundred metres, the shoreline swings right at a reedy bay. Following this shoreline, leave the track to follow a path on the right leading to a headland and then swinging sharply left to climb above some low cliffs, including one protruding rock known as the Devil's Pulpit, best seen from the water. Among them is a crevice called Rob Roy's Cave (not to be confused with the one of the same name on Loch Lomond). Whether Rob Roy used this cave is open to question, but it was certainly frequented by local smugglers—the area was riddled with illicit whisky stills.

The view down the length of Loch Ard now opens out, with Ben Lomond behind. The path leads down to a sheltered bay and swings left, following the shore. Just outside the mouth of the bay on the opposite shore are two huge boulders known as Gog and Magog (two Celtic giants in mythology), and beyond them a chain of tiny rocky islets only a few metres from the shore. The nearest of these, identifiable by a cluster of Scots pines, is called Dundochil and has the remains of the

Craigmore, the Menteith Hills and Aberfoyle from the viewpoint

15th century Duke Murdoch's castle. It must have been a very modest castle, as the islet is only a few paces wide!

The path soon leaves the bay and rejoins the original track where you turn right. At the next junction of tracks, turn sharply left and go uphill through the conifers. After 500m you turn right at the next junction, then left at the next which leads to Lochan a' Ghleann- ain in its picturesque setting.

Lochan a'Ghleannain

Some 200 metres beyond the loch, ignore a track coming in from the right. From this point the most direct route back to the car park is straight down the track you are on, but a far more rewarding way is to leave the track after about 250 metres and follow a path on the left which climbs steeply to the low ridge above you.

As you descend on the other side it is worth pausing at a viewpoint from which you can see Ben Lomond to the west and the Ochil Hills to the east beyond Aberfoyle. To the right of the Ochils on a clear day you can pick out the Wallace Monument and Stirling Castle. Further to the right are the long ridges of the Gargunnock and Fintry Hills, then the dis- tinctive peak of Meikle Bin before the partly hidden Campsie Fells.

Now go down to the forest track below and turn right. The track descends with a view of Craigmore directly ahead, before hairpinning down to join the track you started out on beside the two lochans. Retrace your steps to the car park.

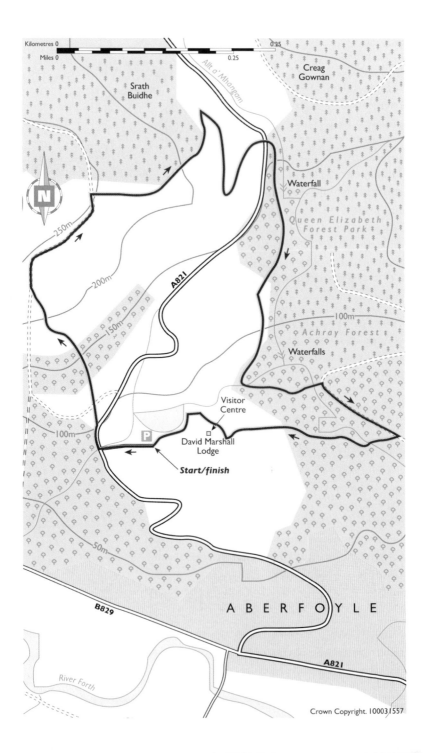

Kilometres 0
Miles 0
0.25
0.25

Creag
Gownan

Srath
Buidhe

Allt a' Mhangom

N

250m

200m

A821

150m

Waterfall

Queen Elizabeth
Forest Park

100m

Achray Forest

100m

Waterfalls

Visitor
Centre

P

David Marshall
Lodge

Start/finish

100m

50m

B829

ABERFOYLE

A821

River Forth

Crown Copyright. 100031557

TROSSACHS TRAMWAYS & WATERFALL WALK

The Queen Elizabeth Forest Park was designated in 1953 and stretches from the east shore of Loch Lomond to Strathyre, encompassing mountains, moorland, lochs, rivers and forest. Although the forest is primarily managed for the purpose of commercial timber production, the Forestry Commission recognises the recreational potential of the area, and much has been done to encourage its use by visitors. Walking and cycling routes have been waymarked and a programme of new path creation began when the Loch Lomond and the Trossachs National Park came into being in 2002.

In a process of forest re-design, the proportion of non-native conifers is being reduced, while indigenous broadleaved species are being encouraged. The result is that more views are opening up within the forest, and sunlight is now reaching watercourses where previously conifers were closely planted.

The Forestry Commission's visitor centre is at the David Marshall Lodge, named after the chairman of the Carnegie Trust which gifted it to the Forestry Commission in 1960. It overlooks Aberfoyle on the A821 road, known as the Duke's Pass (and locally as the 89 bends!). The building was extended in the 1970s and now contains a wealth of information and exhibition material as well as a gift shop and cafeteria.

INFORMATION

Distance: 4km (2.5 miles) circular.

Start and Finish: David Marshall Lodge, 2km north of Aberfoyle on A821.

Terrain: Steep hill paths at first which can be slightly muddy in places, then purpose-built trail. Boots recommended.

Waymarked: In second part.

Refreshments: At David Marshall Lodge.

Toilets: At David Marshall Lodge.

The Visitor Centre at the David Marshall Lodge

Looking down on the Visitor
Centre from the steep section
of the walk

The setting is splendid, and as you gaze south from here across rolling farmland with steep hills behind you to the north, you can appreciate Aberfoyle's position on the Highland Boundary Fault which cuts across Scotland from Arran in the south-west to Stonehaven in the north-east.

A number of waymarked woodland trails start from the lodge, but the short walk described here climbs steeply into open country high above the visitor centre, and returns by the most popular of these—the Waterfall Trail.

To begin the walk, go back through the main entrance and on to the A821 road, cross it and turn right. After some 25 metres you will see a path leading off to the left and forking almost immediately. Ignore this path, but walk on for another 25 metres and take a path leading off to the left, just on the apex of a right-hand bend in the road and heading uphill through the bracken.

After a short distance it crosses a grassy lane, and then a fence a little further up. The gradient now becomes increasingly steep, but splendid views open out behind to give a good excuse for a breather.

Much further up, the path swings right on to an obvious man-made embankment. This is a remnant of the tramway that once brought slate down to Aberfoyle from the quarry further up the Duke's Pass. The trucks ran in a straight line down the steep section, joined by a cable at the top so that the laden ones descending pulled the empty ones back up. Looking downhill you can see the continuation of the line through a cutting, leading eventually to a point behind the primary school.

At the top of the embankment the path levels off, more or less contouring round the hillside. This is still part of the tramway system, and the empty trucks would have been horse-drawn along the gentle gradient back to the quarry. Follow the path for 200 metres, with superb views to the south, until it goes over another embankment and crosses into an area of felled forestry.

Here you leave it and head downhill on a path alongside the edge of the former forestry plantation. This can be a little wet for a short distance, but it soon improves and then joins a well-constructed path leading down to the road.

Cross the road and continue downhill on another good path through lovely birchwoods with a stream over to your left. This path follows the line of an ancient drove route. Further down you will hear the roar of the waterfall, particularly if the stream is in spate.

The path now joins the Waterfall Trail, which is very smoothly surfaced and has a continuous handrail. You turn left on to it to reach the viewpoint at the base of the 18m fall—an impressive sight after heavy rain.

The Waterfall Trail stays on the same side of the stream and loops back to the Visitor Centre, but you can prolong the walk slightly by crossing the footbridge a few metres downstream from here and turning right on to a forestry track. After 200 metres

The small lake in the grounds of the Visitor Centre

re-cross the stream by another footbridge, where the stream narrows and thunders through its channel when in spate.

On the other side of the bridge, climb up a bank and turn right to re-join the Waterfall Trail after 150 metres. Go left, then almost immediately right to return to the Visitor Centre.

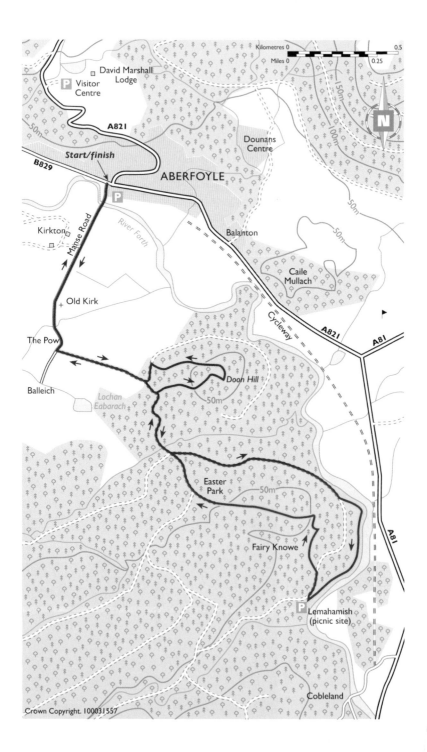

Kilometres 0 _____ 0.5
Miles 0 _____ 0.25

David Marshall Lodge

P Visitor Centre

A821

Dounans Centre

B829

Start/finish

ABERFOYLE

P

Kirkton

River Forth

Balanton

Caile Mullach

Manse Road

Old Kirk

Cycleway

A821

A81

The Pow

Balleich

Doon Hill

Lochan Eabarach

50m

Easter Park

50m

Fairy Knowe

A81

P Lemahamish (picnic site)

Cobleland

Crown Copyright. 100031557

DOON HILL & FAIRY KNOWE

Aberfoyle's claim to be the fairy capital of Scotland focuses around the extraordinary story of its 17th century minister, Reverend Robert Kirk, who was allegedly spirited away by the fairies.

Kirk was born in Aberfoyle in 1644. His academic record was impressive and he went on to become minister at Balquhidder before returning to Aberfoyle in 1685, when he started to take a close interest in the fairy world. Bizarre though this may seem today, it was probably less so in those days when the distinction between religion and the occult was less well defined than now.

Kirk's behaviour, however, was obsessive, and he would go out each night to Doon Hill, an established fairy site, to listen and observe. In 1690, he began his manuscript *The Secret Commonwealth*, a treatise on the fairy world, but on 14 May 1692 he seemingly collapsed on Doon Hill. His body was never found, and although a funeral was held, the coffin was believed to have been filled with stones.

Kirk's wife was pregnant, and he tried to return to human society. He came before a relative, explained how he had become trapped in

INFORMATION

Distance: 8km (5 miles) circular.

Start and finish: Aberfoyle main car park.

Terrain: Paths and forest tracks with occasional muddy sections. Boots not essential.

Waymarked: In places.

Refreshments: Good choice in Aberfoyle.

Toilets: In Aberfoyle, near the Tourist Information Centre.

The old bridge over the Forth at Aberfoyle

The gravestone of the Reverend Robert Kirk

Kirkton Church

fairyland, and gave instructions for the local laird, Graham of Duchray, to await his re-appearance at the baptism of his child. Graham was then to throw a knife over Kirk's head, which would break the spell and free the minister. He did indeed appear, but Graham was so stunned that he failed to carry out the instruction. Kirk left the room and was never seen again.

To retrace his footsteps, walk out of the west end of the main car park in Aberfoyle and cross the River Forth by a fine old stone bridge. You are now in Manse Road, and as you continue along it you can see Doon Hill across the fields to your left. Further on, at the top of a rise just beyond the graveyard, is the Old Kirk. The roof has long since collapsed, but the walls have been restored and you will notice the two iron coffins, one each side of the front entrance. These are 'mortsafes', designed as a safeguard against the practice of bodysnatching for medical research.

Continue along the road for 200 metres to a fork and go left. Beyond the houses, the tarmac finishes and the road becomes a track. Carry on for another 300 metres, and almost at the top of a short rise you will see a sign indicating the Fairy Trail path off to the left, which you follow up through the woods. Further up, as the path steepens, you will see evidence of the conglomerate (puddingstone) rock of which there are numerous outcrops around here.

Very soon you are on the flat top of the hill, where a fine old pine and its smaller companion make a surprising contrast with the surrounding oaks. The larger tree is said to hold the spirit of Reverend Kirk, and the association of the place with this strange legend gives it an atmosphere which more than compensates for the lack of view through the leafy canopy in summer.

To return from the summit a slightly different way, retrace your steps for a few metres and then follow a path more over to the right. This leads down to the foot of the hill and to a forest track where you turn left. After 100m you rejoin the track which you left to climb the hill. If you wish to shorten the walk you can turn right to return to Aberfoyle.

To continue the full walk, turn left, go up the rise and down the other side. The track crosses a small stream just before a crossroads of tracks where you take the left branch. Soon the Menteith Hills come into view over to your left.

Some distance on, the track briefly runs close to the River Forth and then turns away from it to the right. Now look out for a path on the left and follow it along the riverbank. After 500m, the path rejoins the forest track at a small car parking area. The way back from here is to the right, but you may wish to cross a small bridge to Lemahamish picnic area with its stony little beach at a bend in the river.

Bluebells on the path to
Fairy Knowe

To return to Aberfoyle, go back along the forest track, and about 70m past the car park area, take a path on the left. The path slants up Fairy Knowe and further on winds up through lovely oakwoods. In late spring this hillside is beautifully carpeted with bluebells. From the level summit there are views over to Craigmore before the path descends into the woods to join a forest track after a few hundred metres. Here you ignore a path leading off sharp right, but follow the forest track downhill to the same crossroads of tracks you came to earlier on.

You go straight across here and retrace your steps back to Aberfoyle.

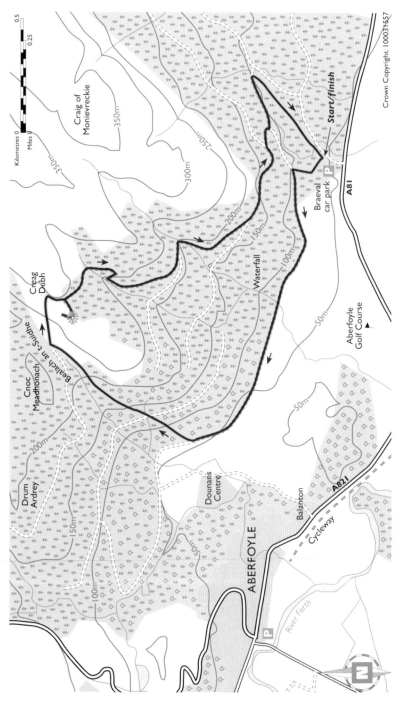

Kilometres 0   0.25   0.5
Miles 0

Craig of
Monievreckie

350m

350m

300m

250m

200m

150m

100m

Creag
Dubh

Bealach an t-Suidhe

Cnoc
Meadhronach

Drum
Ardrey

200m

150m

100m

50m

50m

Waterfall

Start/finish

Braeval car park

A81

Aberfoyle
Golf Course

Dounans
Centre

ABERFOYLE

Balanton

A821

Cycleway

River Forth

N

LIME CRAIG

About 1km after leaving Aberfoyle to the south-east on the A821, the road forks by the Rob Roy Motel. Take the left branch, signed to Stirling, and after a further kilometre turn left into the Forestry Commission car park at Braeval. The larger parking area is on the left, and from its higher level two paths lead up through the trees from the same point.

Take the left path, climb steeply to reach a forestry track after some 300m and turn left on to it. You are now walking just above Aberfoyle golf course. Within a few metres you come out of the forestry and lovely views open out to the south and west. Ahead of you and to the left Doon Hill (Walk 16) is easily identified by the conspicuous crown of the famous old pine tree on its summit, standing proud of the surrounding oak canopy. Ben Lomond dominates the view directly ahead.

After about 1km you reach the end of the golf course, and further ahead you will see a cluster of timber chalets. This is Dounan's Camp, a residential outdoor centre, and in a short distance a track leads down to it off to the left. Ignoring

INFORMATION

Distance: 7km (4.5 miles) circular.

Start and finish: Braeval Car Park, 2km east of Aberfoyle on A81.

Terrain: Good paths and forest tracks, but with a steep ascent to the top.

Waymarked: In places.

Refreshments: Good choice in Aberfoyle.

Toilets: In Aberfoyle, near the Tourist Information Centre.

The track above Aberfoyle golf course with Ben Lomond in the distance

this, you carry on for about 80m and then leave the track to take an obvious path leading steeply up to the right.

Although you are now re-entering the forest, the trees here are mainly larches and sufficiently thinly spaced not to block the view. Across to your left the David Marshall Lodge (the Forestry Commission Visitor Centre) is perched high on a knoll above Aberfoyle, with the bulk of Craigmore behind.

The path on the trackbed of the old wagonway

The steep, straight path you are on runs along the trackbed of an old inclined railway built in the early 19th century to transport limestone from the quarry just below the hill's summit to kilns at its foot. Wooden trucks would have been used, linked by a cable running through a braking system at the top, so that descending laden trucks would pull the empty ones back up. Only three rails would have been needed for most of the way —ascending and descending trucks would share the centre rail. In the middle an extra rail would be added for a short distance to form two sets of double rails as a passing loop.

You emerge from the trees at the old quarry. The limestone appears to run 5km from here to the southern shore of Loch Venachar, in a seam lying west of the distinctive conglomerate or 'puddingstone' rock which is plainly visible in the quarry. The stone was apparently of good quality and is known to have been worked here by 1724, but by the mid 19th century the quarry had fallen into disuse.

Now follow the path steeply up. The summit of Ben Ledi appears ahead looking quite rounded from this angle, with Ben Vane to its left. Much further to the left, the more shapely top of Ben Venue comes into view. The path hairpins right, shortly joining a forestry track which sweeps round to the summit.

The view is very extensive, interrupted only to the east by the nearby higher tops of the Menteith Hills. To the right of Ben Ledi you can glimpse Loch Venachar and to its left the Glen Finglas reservoir. Further to the left the twin peaks in the distance are Stobinian and Ben More—at well over 1100m each they are the highest in the Loch Lomond and the Trossachs National Park.

Return by the track you joined near the summit, now staying on it as it winds back into the trees. The gradient is even and comfortable, and much thinning has taken place in the forest, so that for the most part you can enjoy fine views. Ignore a track coming in at an acute angle from the right just before you cross a stream, and a second one at a similar angle also from the right some way down. Further down still, ignore a steeply rising track to the left, and just beyond it turn left at a junction.

Looking south across rolling farmland to the distant Campsie Fells

About 200 metres further on, look out for a path at an acute angle on your right, which leads you back to your starting point. It hardly matters if you miss it, as you can turn right at the next junction which has a sign pointing back to the car park.

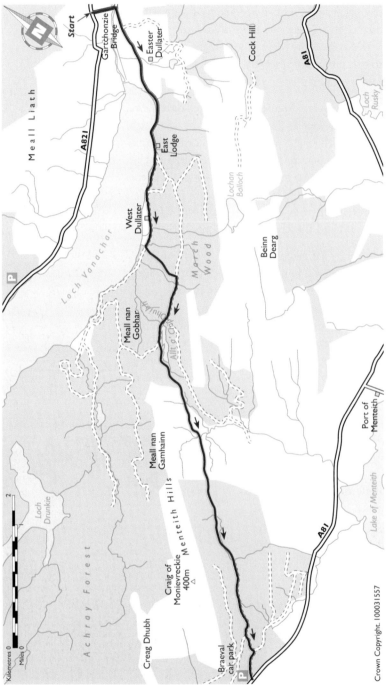

Crown Copyright. 100031557

THE MENTEITH HILLS

This walk can be extended to provide a link between Callander and Aberfoyle, but in order to shorten it and reduce the amount of walking on public roads, the version described here starts 2km west of Callander and ends 2km east of Aberfoyle.

As it is a linear walk, transport is required, and this is provided by the Trossachs Trundler bus service which in summer follows a circular route linking Aberfoyle, Callander, Brig o'Turk and Trossachs Pier. In winter a reduced service is operated, and it is necessary to check the timetable in advance.

The walk is described in a north-east to south-west direction, as parking is better at the southern end, and at the time of writing the Trundler timetable favours that choice. But the views are perhaps better going the other way, and those with their own transport arrangements might prefer to do the walk in a north-easterly direction.

Park at the Forestry Commission car park at Braeval, 1km east of the Rob Roy road junction,

INFORMATION

Distance: 11km (6 miles) linear.

Start and finish: Braeval car park, 2km east of Aberfoyle on A81, for bus pick-up. Begin walking at Gartchonzie road junction, 3km west of Callander on A821.

Terrain: Some tarmac, forestry tracks and generally good hill paths with a few muddy sections.

Waymarked: Yes.

Refreshments: Good choice in both Callander and Aberfoyle, but none on the walk.

Toilets: In Callander and Aberfoyle, but none on the walk.

Picnic spot at the eastern end of Loch Venachar with Ben Venue in the distance

A stream on the moor with the main spine of the Menteith Hills behind

itself 1 km east of Aberfoyle. This is not an official bus stop but the Trundler will pick you up if a clear signal is given to the driver. Get off the bus at the Gartchonzie road junction, just over 1 km south-west of Kilmahog on the A821.

Walk down the minor road, signposted to Invertrossachs. In a few hundred metres at the bottom of the hill, cross a hump-backed bridge and immediately turn right at a junction. After 1 km you come to the eastern end of Loch Venachar and continue along its southern shore. The public road ends shortly at East Lodge, but walkers and cyclists can continue—in fact, this is part of National Cycle Route 7. You carry on past the sailing club and then rise gently to West Dullater, which offers a superb view of the loch. The mountain opposite is Ben Ledi, and beyond the head of the loch over to the west is Ben Venue.

The road descends from here, and after a few hundred metres, look out for a footpath signed to Aberfoyle on the left just beyond a speed hump. Follow the path—it is rather indistinct at first as it crosses a small area of open ground surrounded by woodland, but if you keep over to the left near the edge of the trees you will soon locate it as it becomes more obvious higher up.

The path now climbs quite steeply to enter a conifer plantation. This section is very enclosed by trees, but after 500m or so you emerge from the densest part of the plantation and climb to a small loch where the path briefly joins a forestry track. *If you are doing the walk in reverse, this junction is the only place where you need to keep a look-out for the path.* You follow this track uphill for 100 metres, then leave it where the path resumes on the left to descend to the loch. At this point, however, it is worth walking up to a picnic table on your right to admire the view of Loch Venachar and over to Ben Ledi, which now looks its full height.

Returning to the path, follow it down to the loch, beyond which the forestry gradually thins out until you cross a stile to emerge on to open ground. There is now a great feeling of space as you cross the open moor on a firm path, with the line of the Menteith Hills over to your right.

At the far end of the moor the path re-enters the forest by another stile, but the planting is fairly thin and you are walking close beneath the steep ramparts of the Menteith Hills. After 1km the path ends where you cross another stile to continue on a forestry track. This leads after another kilometre to a junction of tracks where you keep left. In a short distance at the next intersection, go right to follow the track down to Braeval car park.

Looking north
across the moor

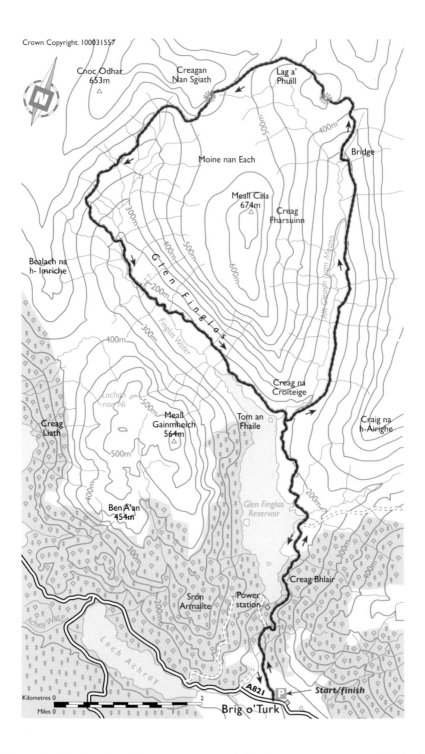

Crown Copyright. 100031557

Cnoc Odhar
653m

Creagan
Nan Sgiath

Lag a'
Phuill

Bridge

Moine nan Each

Meall Cala
674m

Creag
Fharsuinn

500m

400m

Bealach na
h- Imriche

300m

400m

500m

600m

Glen Finglas

200m

Finglas Water

300m

Allt Gleann nam Meann

400m

Creag
Liath

Lochan
nan Ni

Meall
Gainmheich
564m

500m

500m

Tom an
Fhaile

Creag na
Croiteige

Craig na
h-Airighe

200m

400m

Ben A'an
454m

300m

Glen Finglas
Reservoir

200m

Creag Bhlair

300m

400m

Achray Water

Sron
Armailte

Power
station

Loch Achray

Kilometres 0   2

Miles 0   1

A821

P

Start/finish

Brig o'Turk

GLEN FINGLAS

This walk is the longest in the book, and as it climbs to nearly 600 metres in remote country, it is probably the most challenging. However, it follows a clear land-rover track all the way round and unless this is obliterated by snow, navigation should pose no problems.

The Glen Finglas estate was purchased by the Woodland Trust in 1996. At 4,000 hectares it is the Trust's largest acquisition, and an ambitious programme of native woodland restoration is now in hand. The long-term aim is to link the existing fragments of ancient woodland to form what could be one of the largest predominantly native broadleaved forests in Scotland, covering over half the estate.

The project suffered a tragic setback at Easter 2003 when a moorland fire raged across Lendrick Hill above Brig o' Turk. Well over half a million trees had been planted by then, and an estimated 400,000 of these were lost. The area is to be restored, but it takes two years to collect seed and grow on before planting.

The Trust operates a visitor-friendly policy and a network of footpaths has been created around the estate. In due course the intention is to establish another car park to the east of Brig o'Turk. Paths from there will give direct access to the glen, but for the time being visitors are requested to park in Brig o'Turk itself outside the village hall, which is on the right just a few metres from the junction along the Glen Finglas minor road.

INFORMATION

Distance: 23km (14.5 miles) circular, with 500m ascent.

Start and finish: Village Hall car park, Brig o' Turk, 50 metres on right along minor road leading north from A821 junction in village.

Terrain: Tarmac to begin, then land-rover track the rest of the way. A lengthy walk for which at least 6 hours should be allowed. Boots and full waterproofs and windproofs essential, OS Landranger map 57 is advisable as a back-up. Take sufficient food and drink with you.

Waymarked: No.

Refreshments: Tea-room opposite village hall; inn/restaurant 400m to west along A821.

Toilets: None on route.

Glen Finglas reservoir and the peak of Meall Cala

Misty morning in Glen Finglas.

Start the walk by going north along this quiet road through Brig o' Turk and past its old cottages. The name derives from the old Gaelic 'Tuirc', meaning wild boar, which once would have roamed these parts in abundance. The area has inspired writers and artists—in his ballad *Glenfinlas*, Sir Walter Scott tells a tale of seduction in which a hunter falls for the charms of two beautiful maidens dressed in green, and departs into the night with one of them. By daybreak he has been torn apart and devoured—all that remains are his bones, to be discovered in the forest by his companion.

A real-life love-story shocked fashionable society in the 1850s, when John Ruskin, the essayist and critic, spent a holiday in Brig o' Turk with his wife Effie and their friend John Millais, the pre-Raphaelite artist. Millais painted a famous picture of Ruskin standing on rocks by a torrent, but it was obviously Effie who had really caught his eye —the next year the Ruskins' marriage was annulled and Millais married Effie.

About 1 km along the road you come to a fork. The lower branch leads ahead to the Glen Finglas dam, but you take the right branch which winds steeply up through the woods. Where the road levels out there is a wonderful view across the Glen Finglas reservoir, with the peak of Meall Cala beyond. The walk you are embarking on will take you in a circuit right round the back of this hill. The reservoir itself was created in the 1960s as a feeder for Loch Katrine to supply water to Glasgow, but serves a secondary function as a source of hydroelectric power.

Continue along the road through birchwoods. Shortly after the trees thin out, you pass some farm buildings beyond which the tarmac ends and the road becomes a land-rover track, climbing steeply above the reservoir. Just past the highest point of this section a conveniently placed log provides a good seat from where to admire the view into Glen Finglas. The track by which you will descend on your return is visible way beyond the end of the reservoir, while directly behind you is Ben Ledi.

The track now drops towards the shore, and where it comes level with the tiny island of Tom an Fhaile, turn right at a fork, signposted to Balquhidder. You are now entering Gleann nam Meann, steeply at first with the slopes of Ben Vane ahead, but the gradient soon eases as you pass through scattered remnants of ancient woodland with alders predominant. This is a lovely section of the walk, with tree-fringed burns tumbling down from the right, and an increasing sense of remoteness as you continue through the glen.

About 4km from the point where you left the reservoir, you cross a small bridge. Immediately swing sharply right to climb very steeply for a while above the stream. The view opens out behind, and you have a brief glimpse of the far end of the reservoir before the gradient eases and the track rises more gently to a wide expanse of moorland— impressive in its sheer desolation. Except for the track itself there is little evidence of human activity here.

As you cross the moor, the twin summits of Stobinian and Ben More come into view to the north-west, while to the east Ben Vorlich and Stuc a' Chroin appear above the skyline as the track slants up the flank of Carn Dubh. You may be forgiven for thinking that the ascent is never going to end, but it is not far now to the highest point on the track, marked by a cairn.

From here, Meall Cala looks considerably less impressive than it did from the reservoir, as you are now not much lower than its summit. The intervening tract of peaty ground is known as the Moine nan Each, which means the Horse Moss. The story goes that a ghillie attempted a short cut across here in foul weather with his pony, having been sent out to retrieve a stag shot by a royal hunting party. The pony fell into a bog, and with the weight of the stag on its back, could not escape and sank without trace. The ghillie survived to tell the tale, but it is said that the ghost of the pony can sometimes be seen galloping across the Glen Finglas hills.

On a clear day, the views from here extend well into the Southern Uplands, but as you begin the descent, Ben Venue and Ben Lomond soon appear ahead at much closer quarters. You plunge down steeply for a while before the track levels out to contour around the upper reaches of Glen Finglas. The reservoir now comes into view again, then the track swings left to descend to the floor of the glen where it crosses the Finglas Water by a footbridge and follows the stream closely for about 1km.

This gentle section of the walk along the Finglas Water contrasts with the exposed moorland you have left behind, and on a warm afternoon you will no doubt welcome the shade offered by the trees. The woodland here is similar to that in

Gleann nan Meann, but rather more trees have remained here in Glen Finglas.

The survival of these fragments of ancient woodland probably owes much to the fact that the area was used as a royal hunting forest, so that at a time when much of the country was being deforested, the woodlands were accorded special status and properly maintained. As the hunting declined, the trees were recognised as a valuable source of fuel and 'leaf hay' by the agricultural population which moved in, and there is evidence of pollarding on the old alders and hazels, some of which are over 300 years old.

Up to 100 people are believed to have lived in the glen by the mid-18th century, and their livestock would graze among the trees. This is one of the largest remaining examples of upland woodland pas-ture in Britain, and the Woodland Trust's policy is to allow the ground to continue to support sheep and cattle, but with numbers and range of movement controlled so as to avoid compromising the wood-land re-generation programme through overgrazing.

From upper Glen Finglas, looking down on the reservoir and beyond to Ben Ledi and Stuc Odhar

Just after the track leaves the riverbank, ignore a branch track on the right leading to a sheepfold and continue to climb away from the floor of the glen for a while, before dropping down to the shore of the reservoir close to its tip. A grassy knoll just at this point is a good place to sit and enjoy the view.

From here it is about 1km to the junction with Gleann nan Meann, from where you retrace your steps for 5km back to Brig o' Turk.

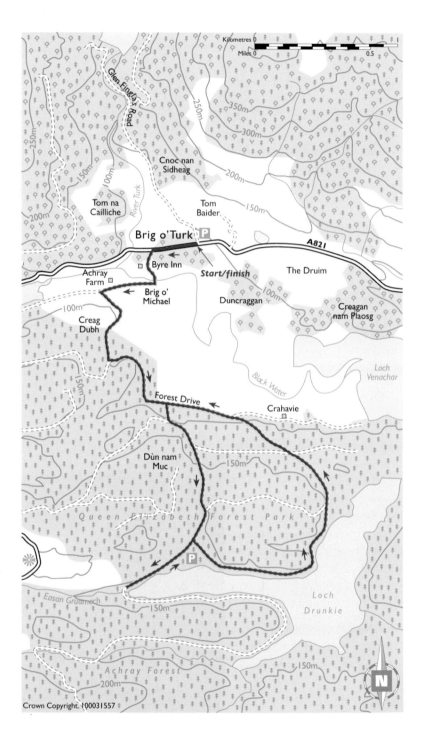

Kilometres 0
Miles 0
0.5

Glen Finglas Road

Cnoc nan Sidheag

River Turk

250m
350m
300m
250m
200m
150m
100m

Tom na Cailliche

Tom Baider

150m

Brig o'Turk
P
A821

Byre Inn
Start/finish
The Druim

Achray Farm

Brig o' Michael

Duncraggan

Creagan nam Plaosg

100m

Creag Dubh

Black Water

Loch Venachar

Forest Drive

Crahavie

150m

Dùn nam Muc

150m

Queen   Elizabeth   Forest   Park

P

Loch Drunkie

Easan Gruamach

150m

Achray Forest

200m

150m

Crown Copyright. 100031557

N

LOCH DRUNKIE

Brig o'Turk is an attractive little place with a long history, as is explained on the information board at the parking area. The 'Turk' of the name is not an exotic immigrant but an anglicising of the Gaelic 'tuirc' meaning a wild boar, and indeed this creature features on the village signs.

From the hall, return to the main road, turn right and take the second turning on the left, signposted for the Byre Inn. The inn is just on the right if you need refreshments. Continue along the track to cross the attractive Brig o'Michael, an old stone arched bridge over the Black Water.

Turn right and walk along to Achray Farm. Go through the gate and at the track junction, turn left. You are now on a popular cyclepath and also on the Forest Drive, so you will have both bikes and cars to watch out for. To the right is a fine view over Loch Achray to Ben Venue (Walk 13).

Go through a gate at a cattle grid and enter the forest. The track is lined with foxgloves in summer. Follow the track round to the left, and at the next junction turn left.

INFORMATION

Distance: 6.5km (4 miles) circular.

Start and finish: Brig o' Turk. There are parking spaces at the village hall, opposite the tearoom.

Terrain: Generally good tracks. Some wet patches. Boots or strong shoes recommended.

Waymarked: Partly, as a cyclepath.

Refreshments: Inn and tearoom in Brig o' Turk.

Toilets: At Loch Drunkie.

A quiet picnic spot beside Loch Drunkie

The southern end of
Loch Drunkie

In about 150 metres take the lesser track on the right (where the tall conifers start), and climb steadily. At a fork go left, still climbing. This track is also a mountain bike route and can be wet in places. Pass over the flank of Dun nam Muc. This continues the porcine theme, as 'muc' (or sometimes 'muick') is Gaelic for a pig, and this is 'the fort of the pig'. The origin of this curious name can only be guessed at.

The track levels out through younger plantations and then starts to descend. Meet a broader track and turn right. You have now rejoined the Forest Drive. Reach a parking area with toilets, an information board and a children's slide, which looks a little odd here in the forest.

The next section of the walk is close to Loch Drunkie. It is a very attractive loch deep in the woods here, but the views of it are frustratingly screened by trees in summer. For a better view it is worth walking down the main track to the right for about 200 metres, where a long view of the loch opens up. The name, of course, has nothing to do with alcohol, but may possibly be derived from roots meaning 'field on the ridge'.

Walk back up the hill, go past the toilets, through the first barrier and take the right fork, a path which leads down to a shelf overlooking Loch Drunkie. This is a lovely walk above the loch—if only the views could be opened out a bit it would be even nicer.

Follow the path for about 600 metres, curving left at a bend in the loch. Drunkie is impounded by a dam as part of the water gathering system that also includes Loch Katrine. At a junction, go right, still close to the loch. The Pine Ridge Walk (red markers) goes left here, back to the parking area.

The path begins to climb and swing away from the loch. In another 150 metres or so you rejoin the Forest Drive. It is possible to scramble down through the trees to the edge of the loch here and get a better view of its upper part.

Continue along the Forest Drive. Before long, a grand view of the hills to the north opens up, with Ben Vane (middle hill, more properly in Gaelic 'Mheadhoin') ahead and Stuc Odhar (dun-coloured hill) to the right, with the top of Ben Ledi peeping over its shoulder.

The track goes gently downhill and round to the left. Keep with it as it swings round several bends, continuing to descend and giving very easy walking. The cone of Ben A'an (Walk 12) briefly comes into view over the trees, and the cycle track to Callander followed on Walk 21 is soon visible down to the right.

Pass the junction with this track, and get a better view of Ben A'an ahead, at a parking area with an information board explaining how the Black Water Marshes are managed for plantlife such as bog myrtle, and for the wildfowl that come here in winter.

Soon rejoin the outward route and retrace your steps back to Achray Farm and Brig o'Turk. If you wanted to extend the walk, you could turn left just before the farm, staying on the Forest Drive to the picnic area beside Loch Achray and enjoying the views up to Ben Venue. This would add about 2km to the total distance.

A peaceful backwater of Loch Drunkie

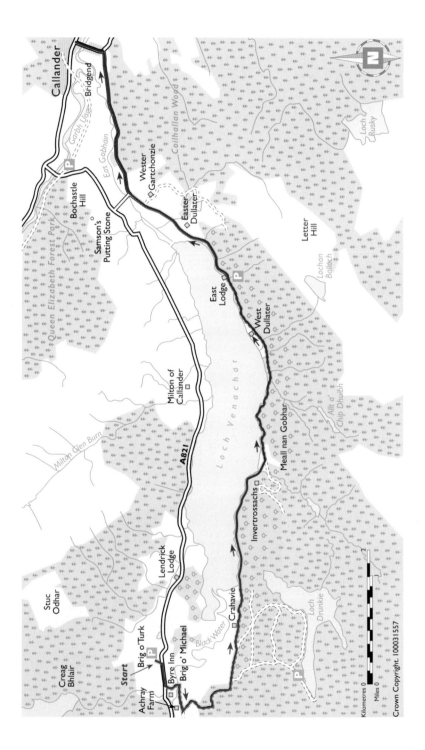

Crown Copyright. 100031557

BRIG O' TURK TO CALLANDER

There is a particular appeal in walking from place to place, and this walk links Brig o'Turk with Callander. It is best to park in Callander and get to Brig o'Turk by using the excellent Trossachs Trundler bus service. You can get the timetable from the tourist information centre. At the time of writing (summer 2004), the Trundler ran all year round, with a reduced service in winter, but it is worth checking times with the tourist information centre.

The first part of the walk is the same as Walk 20. From the bus stop in Brig o'Turk, continue along the road past the tearoom and take the second turning on the left, signposted for the Byre Inn. The inn is just on the right if you need refreshments. Continue along the track to cross the attractive Brig o'Michael, an old stone arched bridge over the Black Water.

Turn right and walk along to Achray Farm. Go through the gate and at the track junction, turn left. You are now on a popular cyclepath and also on the Forest Drive, so you will have both bikes and cars to watch out for. To the right is a fine view over Loch Achray to Ben Venue (Walk 13).

Go through a gate at a cattle grid and enter the forest. The track is lined with foxgloves in summer. Follow the track round to the left, and at the next junction turn left. The view to the left opens up, looking across towards Stuc Odhar (dun-coloured hill). At a layby is an information board about the Black Water Marshes, explaining that you can see geese, wigeon and other birds here in winter.

INFORMATION

Distance: 12km (7.5 miles) linear.

Start: Brig o'Turk (see below for bus details).

Finish: Callander.

Terrain: Hard tracks and minor roads. Boots not essential.

Waymarked: Yes, as a cyclepath.

Refreshments: Inn and tearoom in Brig o' Turk. Wide choice in Callander.

Toilets: At the end of the walk only.

National Cycle Route mile post

Soon fork left, away from the forest drive, at a cycleway sign. This is a relatively new route providing easier access to Callander. Before long you get your first glimpse of Loch Venachar (the horned loch) ahead. Reach the loch shore and pass through a gateway in a stone dyke. You have now entered the large Invertrossachs Estate.

At a fork, stay left, by the lochside. There are plenty of places to sit by the loch if you need a rest. The track winds along, fairly flat and never straight for too long. After a while the track narrows to a path right next to the loch, and there are several small benches.

Reach the policies of Invertrossachs House, colourful with rhododendrons in spring, and cross a footbridge next to an attractive small pond. Go through a gate onto the tarmac road and turn left. Invertrossachs House is hidden in the trees to the right. Queen Victoria stayed here for a week in September 1869, and made a number of excursions which she described in great detail in her diary. She talks of the house as being "small and comfortable"—in comparison to Balmoral, perhaps!

The road is followed for about 5km, but for most of this distance the traffic is very light. A wide view of the loch opens out, and soaring opposite is Ben Ledi. Pass a National Cycle Route milepost saying 'Callander 4' and climb steadily, passing a Girl Guides expedition centre to reach West Dullater with very pretty wild roses outside.

The road drops down to the lochside again, passing the Loch Venachar Sailing Club and finally leaving Invertrossachs Estate at the East Lodge, guarded by two splendid stone lions. Pass a small parking area with an information board. The road is now a little busier.

Reach East Dullater, with the Eas Gobhain (Smith's River) visible to the left, then pass West Gartchonzie which has an organic produce sign. At the road junction ahead, there is a choice of routes.

You can turn left here, over the attractive stone bridge, walk up to the main road and turn right along it for about a kilometre. This would bring you to the point near the Lade Inn where you pick up the cyclepath from Strathyre. Turn right here and walk back into Callander (fuller description in Walk 24).

Alternatively, you can go straight ahead and follow the minor road along. If you walk this way, you soon get a fine view to the left of Bochastle Hill and the enormous erratic boulder known as Samson's Putting Stone.

Pass the Trossachs Backpackers hostel and continue past Callander Holiday Park, a well-laid out site for caravans. There are lots of wild flowers in the hedges in summer.

Callander comes into view, and you reach pavement at the 30mph sign. Turn left at the junction and walk along Bridgend. Cross the bridge over what is now the River Teith. You can either continue up the road into the town, or turn left just after the bridge to walk through the Meadows car park.

Wild roses at West Dullater

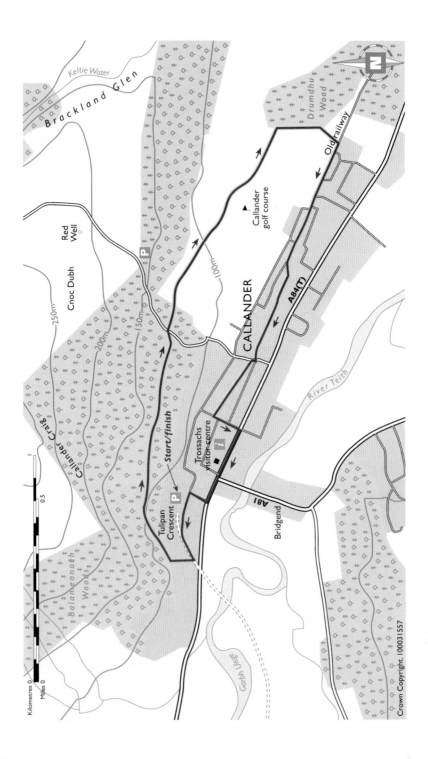

Crown Copyright. 100031557

CALLANDER WOODS & GOLF COURSE

There are a handful of towns in Scotland which boast the nickname 'Gateway to the Highlands'. Callander's claim is more than justified. This fine town, beautifully situated at the junction of the River Teith with the Leny, has long been popular as a tourist resort and indeed as a centre for exploring the hills and lochs of the southern Highlands. Indeed it's been claimed that Callander has, in proportion to its population, the largest number of hotels and guest houses of any town in Scotland. In the 1960s it recieved much prominence as the town where the original series of the popular television programme, *Dr Finlay's Casebook*, was filmed, and in recent years its proximity to the highly populated central belt has made it very popular among day trippers.

Despite its popularity with those who want to visit the Highlands, Callander itself is very much a lowland town. It consists of a long, broad main street from which narrower streets and lanes run south towards the River Teith which forms its southern boundary. The first bridge across the river was built in 1764 and was replaced by the present bridge in 1907.

INFORMATION

Distance: 7km (4 miles) linear.

Start and finish: Car park on the north side of the main street, next to the Dreadnought Hotel.

Terrain: Mostly on footpaths, some of which can be quite boggy in wet weather. Part of the walk passes the Callander Golf Course, and great care should be taken not to disrupt the play of golfers.

Waymarked: Partly.

Refreshments: Wide choice in Callander.

Toilets: At the start.

River Teith, Callander

Signpost in Callander Woods

Those who dislike crowds will perhaps sympathise with the poet John Keats, who passed through Callander in 1818, describing it as 'vexatiously full of visitors'. The person to blame, of course, was Sir Walter Scott whose novels and writings on the nearby Trossachs, particularly the long romantic poem *The Lady of the Lake*, caught the imagination of the 19th-century public. They flocked to Callander, and to Aberfoyle, to drink in the atmosphere of the Children of the Mist, Rob Roy MacGregor and the Celtic twilight.

This walk offers the visitor a pleasant circuit, making full use of the wonderful woodlands on the north side of the town, as well as its delightful golf course, and the former Stirling-Oban railway.

From the car park, take the signed cyclepath next to the hotel and follow it, jinking right and left, to reach a road, Tulipan Crescent. Continue along this road for about 50 metres, cross and take the broad path leading into the woods. Turn right at the fork.

Follow the well-graded path through the lower woods, climbing gently with mainly deciduous trees to your right and conifers on the left. A seat close to a footbridge offers a view westwards towards Loch Venachar. Continue with the main path, now a little narrower and rougher but still quite clear.

After 15-20 minutes of delightful woodland walking, the footpath merges with a surfaced forest road just before a large car park. Go through the car park, turn left onto the Bracklinn Falls road and follow it for about 100m before turning right at a sign which says: 'Walk round Golf Course'.

This is initially a narrow path through bracken. Walk ahead for about 80 metres, turn left and follow a clearer path to a rusting (and redundant) kissing gate. Go round it and stick with the path, to reach the edge of the golf course.

Pass the second tee, and follow the path which leads into the woods again, initially beside an old fence. Cross two burns by footbridges, and follow the path as it leaves the woods and runs out onto the seventh tee. Pass the tee on the left and rejoin the path back into the woods. Take the right fork to pass an attractive small lochan.

Join a wider tractor track and follow it across the 10th fairway, making sure there are no golfers in play. You'll then pass some birches on your right with two Scots pines on your left. Continue straight ahead towards some gorse bushes, again taking care as you cross the fairway, cross to the 14th tee and turn right, heading for a prominent Scots pine (on your left in about 50 metres). Go left when you reach the tree, cross the boundary wall, turn right and follow the wall for about 200m past the 15th tee, with a large landfill site to your left.

Callander Woods

Where the boundary wall turns left, go through an obvious gap in the wall and follow the right-hand path down through some bracken with houses ahead of you. Turn right immediately behind the houses, onto the old railway line. This line has been converted into a cycleway and makes an easy return route, with a fine view towards Ben Ledi and Callander Crags (Walk 23).

Follow the signs along Livingstone Avenue and Murdiston Avenue. The route then becomes a pathway again, passing under the Bracklinn Falls road. At the end of this section, where the cyclepath sign points right, go straight ahead on the footpath between the houses. At its end go right, up steps, and left along the road to return to the car park. Alternatively, you can go left at this point to reach the Rob Roy and Trossachs Visitor Centre and the town itself if you feel in need of refreshments.

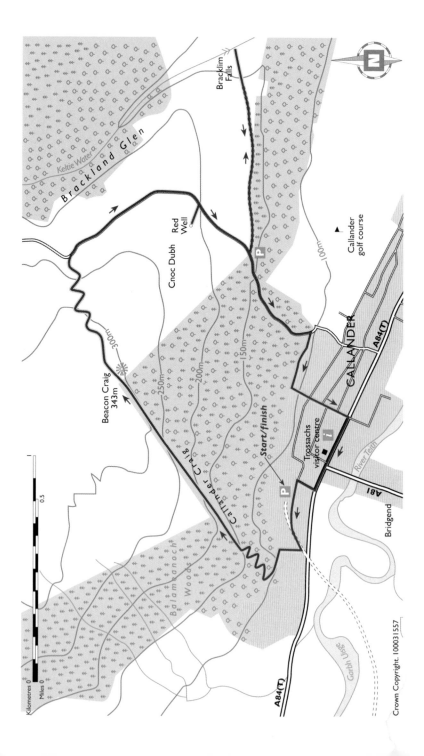

Brackland Glen

Keltie Water

Bracklinn Falls

Red Well

Cnoc Dubh

100m

Callander golf course

P

Beacon Craig 343m

300m

250m

200m

150m

Callander Craig

Start/finish

CALLANDER

A84(T)

P

Trossachs visitor centre

Bridgend

River Teith

A81

Balamacnoch Woods

A84(T)

Garbh Uisge

Kilometres 0   0.5
Miles 0

Crown Copyright. 100031557

CALLANDER CRAGS & BRACKLINN FALLS

The Callander Crags walk has been a popular route with locals and visitors to this Highland border town for generations. To the north-west of the town, the hill rises abruptly and steeply on its wooded slopes, with its bare crags visible through the highest trees. The Bracklinn Falls provide an attractive extra circuit.

The highest point of the Crags, Beacon Craig or, as it is locally known, Willoughby's Craig, rises to a height of 343m. Its ascent, while steep and rough in places, is on a reasonable path and is not too difficult, although there are one or two points near the summit where youngsters should be warned not to stray too close to the edge.

From the car park, take the signed cyclepath next to the hotel and follow it, jinking right and left, to reach a road, Tulipan Crescent. Continue along this road for about 50 metres, cross and take the broad path leading into the woods.

INFORMATION

Distance: 7km (4.5 miles), with 300m ascent.

Start and finish: Car park on the north side of the main street, next to the Dreadnought Hotel.

Terrain: Some steep climbing initially and some exposed drops near to the top of the Crags. Take particular care as you ascend the Crags and near the Bracklinn Falls. Good walking boots are advised.

Waymarked: Partly.

Refreshments: Wide choice in Callander.

Toilets: At the start.

Information board at Bracklinn Falls car park

Bracklinn Falls

At the path fork just inside the woods, go left, and start the climb through some very fine trees. These really are magnificent woodlands, with oaks, chestnuts, beeches and firs mixing with the younger conifers.

The path climbs quite steeply, below the wide green canopy. The path swings round a series of bends as it gains height steadily. Take your time and don't rush it—almost all the climbing on this walk is at the start. There is a seat at one of the bends if you need a rest.

About two-thirds of the way up the hill, just beside a huge double-trunked beech tree, a picnic table on the right overlooks the first viewpoint down to the town and the river. It is a fine view, but is best in winter when the trees are devoid of leaves.

Continue following the footpath uphill under more huge old beeches; near the top of the hill the path becomes a bit rougher and rockier, but take your time, take care, and you won't experience any great difficulty. Cross a burn by a footbridge and continue climbing. The path reaches the edge of the woods, with open ground to the left. A splendid view opens up to the right, looking over the town and the strath beyond. A kissing gate leads out onto the open hill.

The top section of the walk is extremely pleasant, the path climbing gently as it winds its way through birches and pines. Here and there a break in the trees allow you views out over the town of Callander towards the distant Gargunnock and Ochil Hills. But these views are nothing compared to the panorama which opens up as you reach the summit cairn, the Beacon Craig or Willoughby's Craig. Look westwards along the length of silvery Loch Venachar, its head seemingly choked by the high hills of the Trossachs. To its right you look into the very bosom of Ben Ledi, that great wild north-east corrie, and southwards your gaze carries you along the broad strath to Stirling, the Ochils and beyond to the dim outline of the Pentlands south of Edinburgh.

The Red Well

Leave the cairn, built like so many of its kind in 1897 to commemorate Queen Victoria's Diamond Jubilee, and enjoy the descent path through scattered birch, Scots pine and good views over the open moorland. There are a couple of small slabs to get down but no real difficulty. As you descend the final section to the road, the path winds its way through dense scrub birch. Here and there it's a bit tricky to follow, and watch out for slippery roots and boulders.

Turn right and follow the road back towards the town. Just after a right-hand bend you'll come across a signpost on your right, which points out a footpath leading to the Red Well, a mineral spring, about 50-60m off the road. This is a semi-circular stone-built wall with a central plaque embedded in a large stone. Below it a pipe supplies the red ore-coloured water. The plaque contains the message:

THE RED WELL (Chalybeate Spring)
OF OLD TIME REPUTE
RESTORED BY CALLANDER AMENITY
COMMITTEE, APRIL 1924

Return to the road and continue the descent as far as a car park on your left which gives access to a footpath which runs to the Bracklinn Falls, where according to old legend, Sir Walter Scott rode his horse over a rickety bridge for a wager. Follow the path for about 800 metres until you reach a flight of wooden steps leading down to the falls. There

The bridge site at Bracklinn Falls

was an iron bridge here, constructed by the Royal Engineers in 1976 and apparently well above water level, but it was washed away along with several other bridges in the area in the exceptional rains of August 2004. It is hoped that the bridge will be replaced during 2005.

Meanwhile you can still view the falls. It's a grand spot, with the Keltie Water tumbling over a succession of huge sandstone blocks which form a rough, and gigantic, natural staircase. The colouring is rich, with a profusion of mountain ash, oak and beech. A dramatic spot, which so obviously inspired the bard of the Trossachs. Sir Walter Scott, never one to miss a good scene, brought the Bracklinn Falls into his great story, *The Lady of the Lake*:

> As Bracklinn's chasm, so black and steep,
> Receives her roaring linn,
> As the dark caverns of the deep,
> Suck the wild whirlpool in,
> So did the deep and darksome pass,
> Devour the battle's mingled mass.

It's a good description, and none too exaggerated either.

After you've taken in the atmosphere of the falls, make your way back to the car park and the road which descends into Callander. Follow the road downhill, ignoring signs which indicate paths going off on various woodland walks to your right.

About a kilometre from the Bracklinn Falls car park, you'll reach the rear of a large house, Arden House, which has a footpath running down the left of its garden wall. Follow this path past the house, and then past Broomfield House, and it will bring you out on Ancaster Road.

Turn right, and after about 250 metres take the signed cyclepath on the left down to the Main Street, where you will find a good selection of cafes and eating places if you need refreshment. On the way back to the car park you also pass the Rob Roy and The Trossachs Visitor Centre, which has displays on the area, its history and on the National Park of which it is now a part. It is well worth a visit.

The Keltie Water above Bracklinn Falls

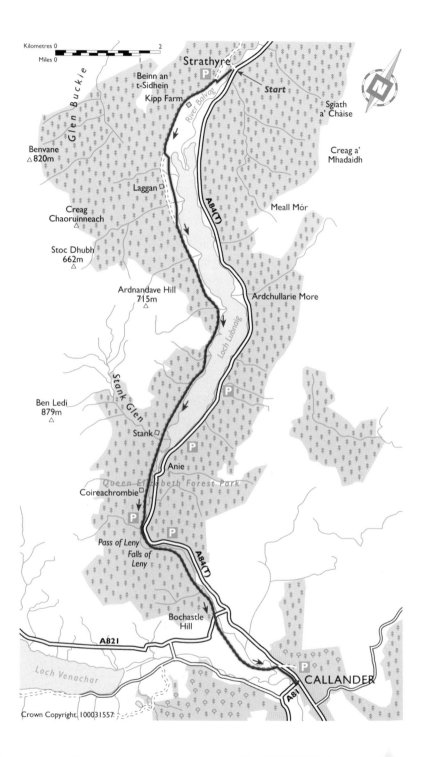

Kilometres 0   2
Miles 0   1

Glen Buckie

Beinn an
t-Sidhein

Strathyre

Start

Kipp Farm

River Balvag

Sgiath
a' Chàise

Benvane
△820m

Creag a'
Mhadaidh

Laggan

A84(T)

Creag
Chaoruinneach
△

Meall Mór

Stoc Dhubh
662m
△

Ardnandave Hill
715m
△

Ardchullarie More

Loch Lubnaig

Stank Glen

Ben Ledi
879m
△

Stank

Anie

Queen Elizabeth Forest Park

Coireachrombie

Pass of Leny
Falls of
Leny

A84(T)

Bochastle
Hill

A821

Loch Venachar

CALLANDER

A81

Crown Copyright. 100031557

STRATHYRE TO CALLANDER

This walk uses part of National Cycle Route 7 to link Strathyre with Callander. It is best to park in Callander and get to Strathyre on a bus. The Citylink service leaving Callander (Station Road) at 11.00 is recommended, as it runs every day. Other bus times can be obtained from the tourist information centre.

From the bus stop in Strathyre, walk through the car park next to the village shop (good selection of drinks, chocolate etc.) and take the path at its left-hand corner, going left behind the houses. Strathyre—the name means 'valley of the Irish'—is an attractive village with good facilities and is worth looking round if you have time.

The path you are on is in fact on the line of the old railway, which closed in 1965, and the houses are on the site of Strathyre Station. I wonder if they ever hear ghostly trains at night?

Cross a burn by a footbridge and continue to cross the River Balvag by a suspension bridge. The path leaves the line of the railway here and goes to the right, up to some forestry houses. Turn right and then left on the road, as signed. There are signposts all along the route but the mileages shown are curiously erratic. The first sign out of Strathyre says 'Callander 8' and the next says 'Callander 8¾', which is a little disheartening!

Follow the road as it climbs gently. Before long you get your first view of Loch Lubnaig and the outliers of Ben Ledi

INFORMATION

Distance: 15km (9.5 miles) linear.

Start: Strathyre (see below for bus details).

Finish: Callander.

Terrain: Firm tracks and minor roads. Boots not essential.

Waymarked: Yes, as a cyclepath.

Refreshments: Reasonable choice in Strathyre. Wide choice in Callander.

Toilets: In Strathyre and Callander.

The Pass of Leny

towering above it to the right. At a fork keep right (the left fork leads down to Kipp Farm). The tarmac ends here and you continue on a broad forest track.

In about 800m there is a lovely view of the loch. Shortly after this, the route leaves the track and heads downhill on a narrow path. Watch carefully for cyclists here. The path zigzags down to rejoin the old railway line. Looking back there is a fine view of Beinn an t-Sidhein, Strathyre's 'fairy hill' (Walk 25).

You now have the north end of the loch on your left. Pass Laggan Farm, leave the old line and turn right and then left on a track through tall conifers with the loch now some way below. Across the loch to the left is Meall Mor (simply 'big hill') and again there is a lovely view looking back to Beinn an-t Sidhein.

At a broad junction of tracks, go left, downhill to rejoin the line of the railway, now a broad forest track. It must have been a beautiful journey trundling up here in a steam train. The track gives easy, level walking. There is a very steep slope to the right with trees seemingly hanging precipitously above you. If you are following the walk on Explorer sheet 365, you have to reverse the whole map at this point, which in any sort of wind can be a precarious business!

Again the signs are erratic—Callander 5½ is followed not long afterwards by Callander 4. The correct distance is somewhere between the two. Pass through a vehicle barrier onto tarmac at the forest cabins. You need to watch carefully for cars on the next stretch. The cabins are a popular holiday spot, and are well designed and appointed.

Forestry cabin

Go through a gate at a cattle grid. Up to the right is Stank Glen. The seemingly unpleasant name comes in fact from a word for a drain or pool. The glen is one of the routes up to (or down from) Ben Ledi, whose name may mean the hill of light or hill of God. It is known that ritual fires were lit on the summit in ancient times to mark the changing seasons.

Pass Stank Farm and cross the Stank Burn. To the left is the end of the loch and the start of the Garbh Uisge (rough water, though it is relatively smooth here). Pass houses and chalets over to the right, at Coireachrombie. To the left, across the river and not easy to see, is a small burial ground and chapel site dedicated to St Bride or St Bridget. She lived in the 5th and 6th centuries AD and is one of the patron saints of Ireland, but she has many sites named after her in Scotland as well.

Cyclists beside the loch

The narrow Pass of Leny is now clear ahead. Reach a barrier at the point where the road goes left, over the river, and carry on straight ahead, leaving the tarmac no doubt with some relief. A sign says Callander 3 (right this time!). Walk through the car parking area and continue on the cyclepath. It is not now following the railway line, which crossed the river at this point.

The path wanders pleasantly along by the river, and after a while the old line comes in again. The line continues in a shallow cutting with tree cover including many fine birches to either side. This hides the Falls of Leny over to the left, a popular short walk from a car park on the A85.

Eventually you reach the road at Kilmahog, with the Lade Inn a little way to the left. The sign here says Callander 1¼ and Strathyre 6 which has chopped over two miles off the correct distance—most peculiar. Cross the road with care and continue under a bridge. The path is now surfaced and is a popular short walk from Callander.

Cross the Bochastle Farm road. On the left is the site of a Roman Fort, with grass mounds clearly visible in the field. After a straight stretch, the path curves left to cross the river on a sturdy bridge. The cycleway goes up and crosses the main road but a nicer route is to leave it just before the road and turn right, following a tarmac park to the Meadows car park and thus back into the town.

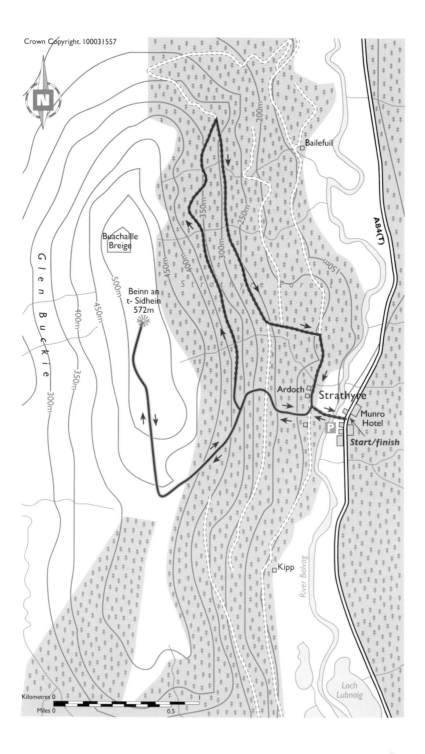

Crown Copyright. 100031557

BEINN AN T-SIDHEIN

Beinn an t-Sidhein, the *Hill of the Faeries*, dominates the village of Strathyre. This small forestry village, the Bonnie Strathyre of the song, lies at the head of Loch Lubnaig on the A85 Callander-Lochearnhead road, and was once known as Nineveh on account of its large number of pubs.

The original crofting village of Strathyre was once on the other side of the River Balvag, but that was lost almost completely when the Callander to Oban railway was built. Time goes on, and now the railway is no more, the original track offering a fine walking route all the way to Callander (see Walk 24).

It would have been a rather strange injustice if, in 1846, the Glasgow Water Company had fulfilled its plan of taking 40 million gallons of water a day from Loch Lubnaig. This would have meant flooding the village of Strathyre. But, in the nick of time, the Company's works were taken over by the then Glasgow Corporation, who decided that Loch Katrine better suited their plans.

This walk offers a steep, but rewarding hill climb, lifting you quickly high above the village with a particularly fine view down the glen over Loch Lubnaig. From the car park, walk north through the village and turn left opposite the Munro Hotel. Cross the bridge over the Balvag, then turn left at the road junction.

INFORMATION

Distance: 10km (6 miles) circular, with 450 metres ascent.

Start and finish: Car park, Strathyre village.

Terrain: A steep climb up Beinn an t-Sidhein, but on a reasonably good path. The loop in the forest is on a good track. Boots recommended.

Waymarked: Partly.

Refreshments: Hotel and tea-room in Strathyre.

Toilets: At the start.

The path through the trees

The start of the path through
the forest

Not far along this road, a footpath leaves the road on the right, and climbs steeply through the trees.

Climb straight uphill and after a while the track bends left, climbs up another steep stretch, and reaches a forest road. Go right onto the road, follow it for 100m, then turn left onto another footpath with a marker post. Keep climbing steadily, with ever-widening views opening up along the valley to Loch Lubnaig and Ben Ledi. Soon you leave the views behind you as you enter the trees again and begin the steepest part of the ascent. It's hard work, but it doesn't last too long.

Near the top of this steep section, a rock slab appears to bar further progress. You can either climb over the slab, or turn it on the left, but take care because there is a steep drop below you. A little further on, a track leads off to the right to Bailefuil. This is part of the return route—for now, take the path which leads off diagonally left. Follow it out of the trees and onto the open moorland. The waymarking stops here. When

Beinn an t-Sidhein from Loch
Lubnaig

you reach the ridge, turn right and follow the path up to the summit of Beinn an t-Sidhein at 572 metres. There is a grand panorama from here.

To the south, the whole of Loch Lubnaig stretches before you in its glaciated valley. To the north-west are the hills beyond Balquhidder, while to the north-east you look towards Lochearnhead, and further east to shapely Stuc a' Chroin. It is a place to linger and enjoy to the full.

When you are ready to return, follow the path back down the ridge and into the forest. This time, when you reach the track leading off to the left and waymarked as a circular walk, turn off and follow it. The track leads through the forest, mostly fairly level, for 2km, giving good views across the glen towards Meall nan Oighreag. It then descends to meet another forest track.

Beinn an t-Sidhein from the south

Turn sharp right here as signed and follow this track for about 1.5km, gradually descending. At a very clear junction, turn left and walk down to the minor road. Turn right along the road, back to the bridge over the Balvag and thus into Strathyre. Taking this route avoids the very steep final section of the hill path.

The forest loop can of course be omitted if you simply want to go back down the hill path into Strathyre. Either way, you will have enjoyed a good walk, and if you chose a clear day, a lovely view taking in a broad sweep of the beautiful Trossachs.

Loch Lubnaig and Ben Ledi from the ridge

INDEX